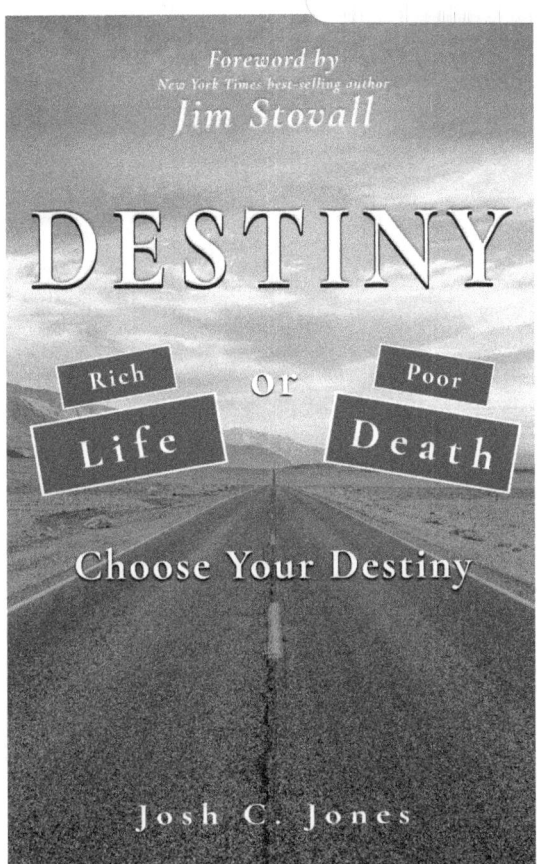

Foreword by
New York Times best-selling author
Jim Stovall

DESTINY

Rich or Poor

Life or Death

Choose Your Destiny

Josh C. Jones

FMS
BOOK

DESTINY:
Rich or Poor,
Life or Death,
Choose Your Destiny

Josh C. Jones

FMS Books

DESTINY:
Rich or Poor, Life or Death,
Choose Your Destiny

ISBN: 979-8-9870614-5-9 (Paperback)
ISBN: 979-8-9870614-6-6 (Ebook)

Second Edition

FMS Books

Cover Art, Editing, Layout and Design by Josh C. Jones.
Cover created using Adobe Photoshop and Coverjig.com
Cover image credit: Johannes Plenio

First Edition, *DESTINY: Life or Death, Choose Your Destiny*, 2020.

All opinions expressed in this book other than the foreword are the author's.

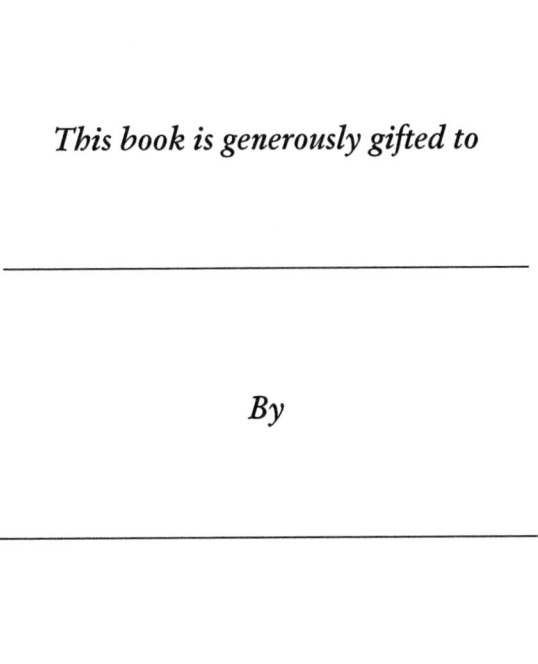

This book is generously gifted to

_____

By

_____

DEDICATION

This book is dedicated to God for the inspiration and passion to write this message, which is my first book, and to my loving family—I thank you so much for all your love and continued support.

FOREWORD

New York Times Bestselling Author,
The Ultimate Gift

Jim Stovall

Foreword by Jim Stovall-

I want to congratulate you for the investment of time and money you are making in this book. Several years ago, there was a study done of Fortune 500 CEOs and self-made millionaires to determine what personal and professional characteristics they had in common. It was discovered that the most prevalent trait among these successful people was the fact that they read motivational, inspirational, and educational books on a daily basis. Not all readers are leaders, but all leaders are readers.

When I first talked with Josh Jones, I realized

very quickly that we shared a passion for delivering very similar messages. Throughout my more than 50 books, nine movies based on them, and over a thousand syndicated columns, my overarching message remains: We all have the right to choose; we are one quality decision away from anything we want; and we change our life when we change our mind.

Within these pages, my friend Josh Jones is going to take you on a journey of discovery. You will discover that you are responsible for your past as well as your current circumstances. However, Josh will also help you discover that you control your future and can confidently pursue the highest calling you feel on your life.

As a former national champion Olympic weightlifter, one of my prized possessions is my gold medal. It is a very special momento to me, which I display in my office. Recently, I was traveling on an airplane, and I met a unique gentleman seated next to me. If they ever add an Olympic event called the Marathon Bad

Attitude, this gentleman will have a gold medal, too.

Shortly after introducing myself, he told me he didn't like the airline we were flying on, the seats, the aisles, or our flight attendant. He went on to inform me he didn't like the city we were in, the airport we were connecting through, or our final destination. I don't think he liked me either, but we didn't get that far into the conversation.

After we took off, our flight attendant told us that we would have a choice of chicken or beef for our dinner. I told her I would enjoy the chicken dinner, and my "Olympian seat mate" told her he didn't care which one he got. She informed him that he was a first-class passenger on this airline and it was her job to make him happy, and they had plenty of both the chicken and the beef, so she would be delighted to bring him whichever one he would prefer. He informed her once again, "It really doesn't matter—just bring me something."

A few moments later she returned with my chicken dinner and gave him the beef dinner. For the next 41 minutes of this flight (I actually timed it on my Braille watch), he told me everything you can imagine, and some things you could not imagine, that was wrong with his beef dinner, and why he wished he had the chicken dinner. I realized that this is the way most people live their lives. There are a few people who make the right decisions, and there are a few people who make the wrong decisions, but the vast majority of people really never make a decision at all. They simply complain about the results. These are people who spend more time planning their three-day weekend than they do planning the rest of their lives.

This life we are living right now is not a practice game. It is the Superbowl, and the World Series, and the Olympics all rolled up into one. If you do not feel that way about your life and what you do, you need to do something different or get a new attitude about the things you do now. Your destiny awaits.

Regardless of who you are and where you are as you begin reading this book, I want you to remember that your past does not dictate your future, and your present circumstance is nothing more than the starting gate for the race of your life. I firmly believe if you will embrace and apply what Josh Jones shares with you in this book, you will find a transformational experience awaiting you within these pages. I'm looking forward to your success.

-Jim Stovall, bestselling author, *The Ultimate Gift*

CONTENTS

"To acknowledge another is the highest form of gratitude, and when we are grateful for others, our focus shifts from selfish thoughts to thoughts of servitude."

Josh C. Jones

ACKNOWLEDGMENTS

Wow! Writing a book is tough; writing your first book is tougher than cutting through Kevlar with a kid's safety scissors. I tip my hat to all who have written a book, published or not, for I now understand the struggles and fears and doubts and enjoyment and this amazing feeling of accomplishment in completing such an intimidating goal—it's a great sense of success.

I would like to thank God first and foremost. Without Him, I would not be here or able to do anything. Without God, I would not have been able to get through the tough times in my life that have helped teach me and grow my character and knowledge and spirit. Everything I am able to accomplish is because of Him.

To my family:

Thank you, Judy B. Jones. Thank you, mom, for all the hours you willingly conceded to give up your rest and HGTV time to graciously sit and listen to me read my drafts to you, and for all the feedback and self-examination role-playing you so accurately performed and acutely knew I needed in order to properly write this book. You are truly a gracious and loving person. I love you, mom!

Thank you, Leonard R. Jones. Thank you, dad, for your continued support in all my ventures. I love you, dad!

Thank you, Christopher R.P. Jones. Thank you, brother, for joining me in some of the ventures that have led to some of the knowledge and understanding needed for this book and others. I love you, brother!

Thank you, Philip W. Wilson. Thank you, Grampy, for all the love and support you have shown throughout this process and to everyone around you. And I thank you for reading the near final draft and giving your expertise on the possible layout of the book for better readability. Your years of service in the photography and printing world has given you an acute awareness of how to best prepare the layout of this book to better fulfill my hopes in providing a material that all can read. I love you, Grampy!

To my friends:

Sean Johnston and Ryan Brandt.

Thank you, Sean, for reading my earliest drafts of Chapter One and for your honest and direct feedback. Without that, I might not have rewritten that chapter or any chapter, and this book definitely would not be what it is today.

And I thank you for sharing your knowledge of English writing to help me with any grammar and sentence structures I may have missed in my editing. I incorporated most of your suggestions.

Thank you, Ryan, for working with me all these years. Our ability to keep each other motivated and encouraged on projects, especially in and with certain meetings, has greatly helped in acquiring the knowledge and understanding needed for the writing of this book.

Thank you:

Thank you to Aaron Jones, the first person who was (at the time of the first edition of this book) currently working in the publishing business and believed in the message within this book. I thank you for not only making my dream come true of being a published author by taking a chance on a first-time author, but for also giving me some of the most encouraging words that an author, let alone an unknown first time-author, could hear when you said you believed this book to be up there with Napolian Hill's *Think and Grow Rich* book, in time, of course.

Thank you, Rick Luttrell, for starting your podcast, which, while we worked on the format for it, gave me the idea of how to analyze my early drafts to find a breakdown on how to make the writing of each chapter a little more bearable for myself. Without this, I'm not too sure this book would have the solid flow from chapter to chapter that it has.

Thank you to Brad Stine and Dr. Dave Leggett. Without you two daring to step out and create the business you did, we would not have met or had the meetings and discussions we did, nor would I have been able to meet many of the other people at those meetings that helped spur some of my writing for this book and others.

Thank you, Dr. Dave Leggett, for standing

with me from the beginning of this venture as an author and for helping me make contact with my first publisher—a privilege and a blessing that I will never forget.

Thank you, Mr. Jim Stovall, for your kindness to meet with me, listen to me, and support me as a writer, and for your interest in and support for this book. It means more to me than you could know to have such an accomplished author, successful entrepreneur, and speaker take the time to talk with me, pass along their wisdom, and go above and beyond writing a powerful foreword for this book. No matter how much I write here, I could never thank you enough. I am grateful beyond words.

"It is in your moments of decision that your destiny is shaped."¹

Tony Robbins

CHAPTER 1

PROLOGUE

O h, that final point of destination, supposedly predetermined by an out-of-this-world force that no one has any hope of developing. You know what I am talking about, right? That is what this book is written about. Our uncontrollable, unwavering, and set in stone destiny. But is it really set in stone? Could we actually have an influence on our destiny? Let me delve into my "professional" tone and further explain.

Destiny, or fate as it is sometimes referred to, is the consequential path to an arranged end based on numerous decisions we make throughout our life. The key takeaway here are the two words "we make." "We make" indicates influence, an influence we have over our lives.

Do you make decisions? Of course you do. Do you make choices? Absolutely. Do you "make up your mind"? Oftentimes, I'm sure we all do. If so, then we have something in common: "We make." And you have made a great choice today by reading this book; because you made the decision to better your tomorrow. As one person wisely said, "The best preparation for tomorrow is doing your best today."[2]

Now, the five traits that will be discussed in this book are not only unique to themselves, but they are intrinsically woven together to create the whole—the whole that has the ability and power to mold our destiny.

The traits listed in this book are, in my opinion, sometimes dangerously neglected in most people's lives—something that, until the preparation and writing of this book, I now knew was neglected in mine. It is through the understanding of each trait, and of the power we hold by making the decision to change our lives to better these traits, that we increase our chances to live a healthier and more joyous and productive life.

For me, the personal discovery of how powerful these traits are and how they work together began years ago in a business meeting. My business partner and I were associates of the organization that was hosting these meetings. This organization helped people and businesses organize and formulate their ideas, or "dreams," into written plans called "Master Plans." The organization, with the help of associates, also helped create videos and photos for the client's "Master Plan" as well as fundraising banquets to begin, or in some cases continue, their work. We had the privilege to meet so many unique people—successful and what the world would consider unsuccessful—happy, sad, stressed, joyful, accomplished, and striving individuals. There were some topics discussed at a few of these meetings that really stuck with me and started my thinking and research in this area.

The discussions we had, the points made, and the experiences and information we learned while helping clients were very intriguing and really made me think about my own situations and mindset in life.

"Could we actually have an influence on our destiny?"

It is amazing how difficult it can be to truly be completely honest with yourself, especially since we know when we are lying or "justifying" things to ourselves. I've always wondered why we think the easiest person to trick is ourselves. We never buy it; we always know, deep down, that we are not being honest. Anyway. It was not easy being honest with myself while digging deeper into these traits and remembering—and in some cases confronting—my memories and the doubt, negativity, and fear in some of these areas. I still have a long way to go, but the understanding I have learned from aspects of my past when analyzed with this information, and the utilization I have applied from this knowledge to certain areas of my life from the start of this writing, have helped me immensely and, I believe, helped redevelop the path of destiny I was on; the previous path was not one I liked or had much joy or hope in—it became bleak, dark, and, well, hopeless, which is very devastating. Without hope, what's the point? The point is that there is hope.

In fact, this isn't the only good book that I return to, but I have referred back to this very book in recent dark valleys and stormy seasons in my life. It has been and will continue to be an important reminder of how we can have an influence on our very destiny and how we can choose ("we make") to change our lives from valleys to mountain tops, from failure to success, from darkness to light. It's amazing to me how we—and it has happened to me many times—can get so wrapped up in the circumstances surrounding our lives that we can begin to lose focus and easily begin to reshape our destiny from that of life to that of death. In these times, there is a big lesson that I have learned: that no matter how strong, intelligent, wise, or secure we think we are, we will all need help from time to time to remind us of the powerful message in those two words, "We make," and to encourage us to not willingly relinquish the control we do have over these five traits. And the time will come in each of our lives where our strength, our faith, and our current understanding of that season will be tested and brought to light.

At one of these meetings, a gentleman said something that brought to my attention the one trait that has the most power and control over our lives when he made this comment: "If you truly want to see what is in someone's heart, just watch what comes out when they get bumped hard and are not expecting it."[3] This comment made me stop and really begin to think about this one trait that has the power to raise our lives to a better state or bury us six feet under.

"Rich or Poor, Life or Death, you get to choose your destiny."

We will be discussing all five traits, but the one I speak of is, I believe, the root of the other four.

Before I continue, I want to let you know of two other really good resources written about the first trait, which is the root, and each book explains the importance and value of understanding and controlling this trait as best we can, but from two differing perspectives. They are not my books, but I do believe they can also be very helpful for you. But, please, finish this one first, because I know you will like this book, and I truly believe this book will be a valuable resource for you. The first one is Joyce Meyer's book titled *Battlefield of the Mind*, which explains this trait from a religious viewpoint, explaining God's wisdom as written in the Holy

Bible and the importance of our choice in this trait and the impact it will have on our lives. The second one is by Dr. Caroline Leaf, who writes about the very same trait, its importance, and how we have the choice to change it for the better, just like Joyce Meyer did, but from the viewpoint of science and verified scientific data, which is titled *Switch on Your Brain*. But I want to take us even further, looking a little more deeply into that first trait, exploring beyond just that first trait, and seeing how what sprouts from this root is also our choice, and how, together, all five of these traits can and will help determine our destiny.

My hope is that you will find this information as intriguing, powerful, and helpful as I have, and that you might find the power endowed upon us through our ability of choice; our freewill. I also hope that you will be able to find more joy, peace, and positivity in your life through this information. Because, through this information, you can improve your chances of success, find more joy in this journey, and change your life.

I have a lot of hope for this book and for you.

Every person has these five traits, and every person has the power to reroute the direction their life is going and change their current place on this journey. In other words, each of us has the power and ability to help guide our destiny.

"The point is that there is hope."

Thanks to the understanding I have gained, partly through the discussions I had with people at those meetings, the contemplation and reflection of past experiences, and the continued inspiration from the research involved in writing this book, I can bring this message to you.

That message is a better understanding of the power we have over our lives and the world around us through choice, a better understanding of why positivity, generosity, and even servanthood are so important in creating our world, and how to become a person of better character so we might have a better destiny.

In short, the purpose of this book is to encourage the conversation and contemplation of the five traits that mold and create our destiny, because each of these five traits is completely controllable, but only if one first realizes the importance of and has the willingness and discipline to admit their power and attempt to mold their lives to better these traits. In other words, we hold the power of choice over our own lives, and that power comes from the personal decision to mold these traits in our favor—"we make."

My hope, I told you I had a lot of hope for you, is that you will be able to learn from the stories and information in this book so that you will not continue to nourish negativity, have to repeat the same valleys that I've been in, or spend years learning the hard way, as I have in some of it.

In reality, you are in charge of the path your destiny takes: rich or poor, life or death.

As Frank Outlaw, the late President of the BI-LO stores, was attributed as stating:

"Watch your thoughts, they become words;

Watch your words, they become actions;

Watch your actions, they become habits;

Watch your habits, they become character;

Watch your character, for it becomes your destiny."[4]

"It takes but one positive thought when given a chance to survive and thrive to overpower an entire army of negative thoughts."

Robert H. Schuller

CHAPTER 2

THOUGHTS

Grandpa Phil was in his seventies and was sporting a thick beard and mustache—not a chest-length beard you would see on those reality shows with duck hunters, but thick enough for him to find crumbs in it from his evening meal late into the night. One afternoon, Grandpa Phil was taking a nap on the living room couch when his grandson thought it would be funny to rub limburger cheese on his mustache; you know, the cheese that smells like the worst foot odor you can imagine. Well, his grandson, as gently as he could to not wake up his grandpa, rubbed it in and waited patiently for him to awake.

When Grandpa Phil awoke, he let out a loud grunt and shouted, "Something stinks in here!"

He then ran around the house, trying to identify the room from which the smell was emanating.

As he ran from room to room, he was shouting, "This room stinks, and this room stinks. They all stink!"

At this point, he became desperate for fresh air that didn't stink like the locker room of a high school football team after a hard-fought victory in the middle of the August heat.

Grandpa Phil ran outside, inhaled deeply, and then looked at the sky and shouted, "The whole world stinks!"

This was similar to a story I heard many years ago that taught us the importance of our thinking. Our view of the world, this journey that is our lives, and of ourselves will be shaped by and mirror the scent we hold in our minds—this scent will create our perception, which will be the lens from which we view, judge, and accept what we and this world are. Just as sweet-smelling aromas fill the rooms of our home and can create a sense of happiness for us in that moment and brighten our day with nostalgic memories, so can good and positive thoughts help create for us a brighter and happier journey in this life. So, if we think negatively, then our world will most likely stink, but if we can change our thoughts to be more positive, then we can change our world for the better.

If you want to change your world, then start at the beginning.

Our mind, our thinking, is the beginning of our destiny. Our thought is the start of the five traits. Thought is the one alluded to in the prologue. Thought is the seed from which all the roots will sprout, and the tree that is our lives will grow, and the fruit will be produced. We will all produce fruit; it is up to each of us individually, though, if our fruit will be ripe or rotten.

Throughout history, many great minds have fully agreed on few things, but one thing that has captured their nearly unanimous agreement is found in the old saying, "We become what we think about."

Marcus Aurelius, the Roman emperor from 161 to 180 AD, is quoted as saying, "Our life is what our thoughts make it."[2] Ralph Waldo Emerson, an American poet and philosopher who lived in the 1800s, said, "A man is what he thinks about all day long."[3] The author of one of the best-selling personal development books, *Think and Grow Rich*, Oliver Napoleon Hill, said, "Whatever your mind can conceive and believe, it can achieve."[4]

We could go on and on about people who, throughout history, believed in and were quoted with similar phrases, all pertaining to the power of our thoughts. That is why I came to this conclusion: if people from different walks of life, from different centuries, and with various beliefs are all talking about and agreeing on one similar idea, then maybe, just maybe, that is an idea worth researching.

"Our mind, our thinking, is the beginning of our destiny."

Our mind is the production house of our world. Our mind is where our thoughts, those essential and often overlooked elements of our daily lives, are born. Our mind is the womb from which our whole world is birthed. Naked we came into this world and naked we shall leave this world, and just like that, our minds are a blank canvas just waiting to be dressed in garments of rags or luxury, whichever we create for them.

So, other than being important and seemingly powerful, what is thought? Pulitzer Prize-winning philosopher and historian Will Durant has a good idea of what thought is. As he wrote in his book *The Greatest Minds and Ideas of All Time*, "What is thought? It baffles description because it includes everything through which it might be defined. It is the most immediate fact that we know, and the last mystery of our being. All other things come to us as it forms, and all human achievements find in it their source and their goal."[5]

Thought includes everything from the past to the present to the unknown future. Everything you see was first created in the mind of someone through their thoughts. Thought is the starting point for all our goals, all our achievements, and all of our formation and deciphering of human communication.

Thought, as defined by Merriam-Webster, is "to form or have in the mind," "reasoning power," and it is also defined as "a personal belief or judgment that is not founded on proof or certainty," and "the content of cognition; the main thing you are thinking about."[6]

So, our thoughts are what we think about in our minds, and they are the result of our perception based on our personal belief or judgment, be it truth or fear-based. Thought is the first place any word, action, belief, habit, or anything we do is created. Thought is the beginning of our lives.

Thought is where the words we speak formulate and where our actions begin. Thought is our conception; it is the birthplace of our lives, and if we are not careful, it can also be the end. As Leon Brown, an outfielder in Major League Baseball, was quoted, "It all begins and ends in your mind. What you give power to has power over you, if you allow it."[7]

Thought, often considered such a small, inconspicuous, and frivolous part of our overall lives, is often overlooked, and yet it is the very place where our attitudes, happiness, life, and world are created. Have you ever wondered why some people, societies, and civilizations censor and attempt to control what people think through what they are allowed to read, hear, watch, see, and/or learn? A free mind set loose to learn outside the box can set in motion a ripple that can renew life and create a whole new world.

Steve Maraboli, who is a world-renowned researcher, motivational speaker, author, and business philanthropist, may have said it best in his book *Life, the Truth, and Being Free* when he said, "Your life is a print-out of your thoughts."[8] I agree with this statement, and this, I think, helps explain why I believe thought is the root and the most important of the five traits that shape our destiny. Thoughts create. They create the words we say, the actions we take, and the habits we live by.

If you're like me, then you are probably thinking Wait! Hold on a second. How can thought be more important than what someone says or does? Words can hurt, words hold power, and people's actions and habits are what actually cause the blessings or curses in their lives. I mean, it is someone's habits that cause them to perform certain actions that affect their lives, right? So how can thought be more important? How can thought be "the root"? Those are some questions I had when I first discovered this concept. But the answer to this is simple. It is because what one says, does, or performs as a habit is first created in the mind, be it consciously or unconsciously. It is based on what was not, and what was not is created in thought. What do I mean by that? Let me start with the saying from Earl Nightingale's *The Strangest Secret*: "You become what you think about all day long."[9]

Yes, I do think words hold a certain power, and that words can and do sometimes hurt. But where were these words first produced? And, yes, I also do think it is true that we are creatures of habit. That habit, however, is produced by the images we hold in our minds of ourselves, our lives, and our own self-limiting abilities. Even though we may be and do what we think, we still have the freedom and ability to choose what we think about. This is how we start to change our lives and shape our destiny. If we cannot first take control of the root, then how can we help control what sprouts from this root?

"Thought is the first place any word, action, belief, habit, or anything we do is created. Thought is the beginning of our lives."

With our thoughts, we create, and one way we communicate our creation is with our words. I'm sure we've all heard a phrase similar to that of Jean-Paul Sartre that "words are more treacherous and powerful than we think."[10] And though this statement is true, my question is: why? Why are words more powerful than we think?

The answer is, once again, a simple one.

Words are more powerful than we think, because oftentimes we don't.

We understand thinking to be good for the use of our knowledge and reasoning abilities in order to make a decision or judgment on someone or something. We typically use our minds to think about how we are going to respond to someone or some situation, be it through words or action, but we rarely stop and think about why we are responding the way we are.

Why do we sometimes, in the heat of the moment, react, respond, or perform a certain habit in a certain situation seemingly instinctively?

Why does one always seem to respond defensively or rudely or apologetically or truthfully or sarcastically with their words?

This makes me think of something from my own past. I spent a few years studying the art of acting for theater and film and learned the importance of breaking down and understanding the character to be portrayed. Why does the character perform a certain action? Why does the character act in a certain way? Why does the character say the words in the script the way I, or the actor, choose to say them? What motivates the character? In other words, what is the character's backstory? This is a fun part of the creative process because what I, or the actor, think about the character, is what will be created and portrayed on the screen or stage. An actor's thoughts create the life of the character. Thoughts create character.

Yet, even after all the training and opportunities to put this into practice—and I had many, though the performances were good they weren't good enough in my opinion—I often felt, while watching myself on film, the words my character spoke just did not seem to always fit just right with the other characters in the scene. Either the pitch, tone, or cadence seemed off—sometimes all three. Then there were the actions in response to the other characters; these, too, sometimes seemed to be the wrong piece in the puzzle that was the story. To me, there was something that always seemed to be missing. The performance didn't always feel realistic and lifelike to me.

It wasn't until I was filming an interview with two acting instructors in 2012 that something finally clicked in my head. One of them said, and I'm paraphrasing because I don't remember the exact words, "Your character, just like yourself, must listen to those on stage you are interacting with."

This got me thinking that if I wanted my character to be real, if I wanted the words to truly fit the character in that moment and the world around them, then I must not just think about my lines, my next line of dialogue in response in the conversation, but I must also listen to what the other person is saying and how they are saying it. Then I could properly think about the response and act accordingly.

I must listen, think, and then respond. This is how I make the character and the acting seem and feel real.

I spoke, but I did not listen or think about what I was saying. In other words, I parroted the words written by the scriptwriter, but I never actually thought like my character would; thus, I merely mirrored someone else's creation rather than using my thoughts to further create the world in which those words lived. This was one major piece that I was missing, and it was a big reason why the performance always fell slightly flat, in my opinion.

Listen. Think. Respond.

How many times do we just respond, without listening or thinking—like a robot preprogrammed to respond in a mindless way? I've done it a lot. I still do it sometimes. We all do. It takes time and work to overcome this. Listen. Think. Respond.

So, where do these words we might respond with originate? Where are they first conceived before making their vibrations known on our vocal chords, traveling on the waves of our tongue, and passing through our Colossus of Rhodes (lips), where we have the power, the choice, to create life or defecate on it?

"Words are more powerful than we think, because oftentimes we don't."

Author Betty J. Eadie, it seems, understood this well when she said, "If we understood the power of our thoughts, we would guard them more closely. If we understood the awesome power of our words, we would prefer silence to almost anything negative. In our thoughts and words, we create our own weaknesses and our own strengths."[11]

Have you thought about your thoughts lately?

According to a 2005 article published in the National Science Foundation, the average person has about twelve thousand to sixty thousand thoughts per day.[12] Seriously? Yes, seriously! Up to sixty thousand thoughts per day! That is about 41 thoughts per minute, or nearly a thought every second. Our mind is a magnificent work of art that is continuously working, continuously active, and continuously creating; but what is it creating? According to the same article, nearly eighty percent of those thoughts are negative. Eighty percent of our thoughts are negative.

Let's pause and think about this for a moment. If all traits start with thought, and eighty percent of our thoughts are negative, then this does not seem like it would bode well for our lives. If it all starts with thought, which is eighty percent negative, and what we think we tend to speak, and we can speak up to sixty thousand words per day, then we might be in for some real rough traveling on this journey called our life. I mean, how many of these words do we actually take the time to consciously and deliberately think about before speaking? How many of these conscious and deliberate thoughts on what to say are positive? According to that article, it is about twenty percent. I think you might agree with me when I say, "I do not like how this is appearing to turn out."

However, this does not have to be the "be all and end all" of our lives. We can change our circumstances, our environment, our attitudes, and our lives by changing our thoughts. We do not have to accept a majority of negative thought processes; we can change our brain and retrain ourselves to think more positively. This is the most important trait, therefore I will repeat myself again: we can change our brain and retrain ourselves to think more positively, thereby creating a better life for ourselves and, hopefully, a better world.

How, you might be asking? Through our conscious and diligent effort—"whatever is true, whatever is noble, whatever is right, whatever is pure, whatever is lovely, whatever is admirable…think about such things."[13] And, most importantly to many people, as proven by science.

Science is a wonderful tool that has both expanded upon itself and corrected itself over the years. Through the science of neuroplasticity, which is the ability of the mind to change the brain, we can positively alter our brain's neurons and synapses through positive thinking.[14] Allow me to explain with a little more detail.

Science once thought that the foundation of our physical reality was Newtonian material, which is a material that exhibits a linear relationship between stress and strain rate. In other words, when stress (force) is applied to a substance, the strain (result) will be consistent. An example would be stirring a cup of water. The water will remain liquid no matter how much stress you apply to it—no matter how fast or slowly you stir it. Science, however, has since discovered that this is not true in all cases. Take oobleck for example. Oobleck is a non-Newtonian substance named after a Dr. Seuss book called *Bartholomew and the Oobleck*. Oobleck is a fascinating substance. This material hardens when heavy stress, or constant movement, is applied and becomes a liquid-like substance when light stress, or slow movement, is applied.[15] This is contrary to Newtonian material.

The contradiction in scientific understanding from Newtonian material to oobleck is just one example of the lack of understanding in our lives when it comes to the five traits and, more importantly, to the power of our thoughts. Our lack of scientific understanding, at least at that time, left us with a semi-false sense of reality, just as our lack of understanding of how important our thinking is to our lives and our future leaves us with a semi-false sense of reality when it comes to the influence our thoughts have on our success and destiny.

After Newtonian material and its contradictory oobleck, science discovered quantum physics, also known as quantum mechanics, which is the study of the physics of the very small and the behavior of photons, electrons, and the particles that make up our world. Quantum physics has found that physical atoms are made of energy that is constantly spinning and vibrating.

"If you want to change your world, then start at the beginning."

According to science, everything, yes, everything, is made of energy. It is all vibrating packets of energy, which then make the electrons, neutrons, and protons that form the atom and so forth, which, in turn, form everything in the known universe.

Early 1900's physicists Niels Bohr and Werner Heisenberg found that physical matter is not "anything" at its most basic and subatomic level. Matter is made of energy, which is made of potentiality. The zero-point field was so named because it found scientists looking at infinitesimal levels of matter and substance and staring at what appeared to be nothing and yet everything. At this place, they found that energy, which was thought to make up everything, is neither energy nor is it an empty space; it appears to be a place of pure consciousness. Bohr and Heisenberg discovered that the act of observation seemed to influence the particles' behavior they were observing.[16]

All these scientific discoveries have since proven that matter is energy, and as it appears thus far, energy is also consciousness, and human consciousness is connected to this energy. This is an eye-opening and new revelation on how we can help shape our destiny: we can change ourselves, our environment, and our lives through the power of our thoughts.

Think about this for a moment: if everything is created from energy, and energy can be created or formed from consciousness, then imagine how powerful our thoughts can be in controlling and influencing our lives. Science shows that matter is made of molecules, which are made of atoms, which are made of electrons, and protons, which are made of quarks, and so on until you get to energy. In other words, energy at its smallest and most condensed level is very powerful, and the more we condense something, the more power we will find in it. If we condense our thoughts to focus on the words we are going to say and why we are saying them (what we wish to create in our lives and the current situation by speaking these words), then we can properly wield tremendous power over our lives.

Take a moment and think about your past. Find that time when you were in a troubling situation—maybe it was an argument with your family or best friend. Whatever it was, you were in a pit; you were in a dark valley. What pushed you into that dark place? What kept you wallowing in despair, self-pity, depression, or hopelessness? Was it the circumstances around you, or was it your negative thinking? Or, in the case of an argument, what was it that escalated the argument and tension? What was it that kept adding the fuel required for such a heated and fiery controversy? Was it the actual deed perpetrated, or maybe a deed one was at least suspected of committing? Or, was it the defensive, prideful, and/or disdainful words that left your mouth in the passion of the moment?

One moment of careful thought, of deliberate contemplation before speaking, could prevent such a long and painful argument. There is a Russian proverb that says this best: "A spoken word is not a sparrow. Once it flies out, you can't catch it."[17]

These words, which we allow to roll off our tongue and pass from our mouth, are the breath of creation. If we allow them to pass without a thought to their intention or consequence, they could have the power to erase all that we have sacrificed and bled to create.

"When a person is emotionally struggling, one word could change their world."

As the British author Rudyard Kipling once said, "Words are, of course, the most powerful drug used by mankind."[18]

The production warehouse of such a drug is in our mind; it is our thoughts.

Entering a forest unknown;

Enchanted this forest you see,

Undeveloped yet full grown,

Unaware what it will be.

Enchanted this forest you see

Infested with trails of thought,

Unaware what it will be,

To visit there is no cost.

Infested with trails of thought,

Winding through thick mist.

To visit there is no cost,

To live here would be bliss.

Winding through thick mist,

Visited by the past,

To live here would be bliss

But it could never last.

Negative thoughts cloud judgment,

Positive thoughts create.[19]

So, what is it that you are creating?

What are you constantly allowing to invade your thoughts?

What is it that you are allowing to enter your mind and then roll off your tongue?

What are you meditating on, reviewing, and allowing to enter your mind?

What destiny are you choosing to create with your thoughts?

Our thoughts are so powerful that they are what control our beliefs. How is this possible? It is possible through the habit of thought—what we think over and over and over again. This habit of thought, through repetition, helps create and shape our beliefs. "As water reflects the face, so one's life reflects the heart."[20] Now, the word "heart" is not just emotions, as we would typically think, but it has also been used to refer to our mind, or thoughts; however, it is also used to encompass our mind, emotion, and will. For in our mind we take action in creating, with our emotion we react to our thoughts, and with our will we make our decision to enrich or pollute. Our thoughts create, and our habits of thought help form. According to neurological research, over ninety percent of our behavior is automatic.[21] Our beliefs are part of this non-conscious automatic behavior formed in our minds through our habits of thought.

As Dr. Dave Leggett mentioned in one meeting, "If you truly want to see what is in someone's heart, just watch what comes out when they get bumped hard and are not expecting it."[22]

These are the times when we will truly know what is in our hearts and minds. What comes out of the mouth comes from the heart, and what one continues to think in his heart, he will become. This does not mean we have always believed what we might say about someone or some situations when said in the heat of the moment, but it was what we chose to allow to enter our minds and what we were thinking when the moment came to pass.

Something interesting for us to think about is this: We speak to ourselves more than we speak to anyone else. Our internal monologue is almost always speaking to us.

So, what are you telling yourself?

Are your thoughts and words encouraging?

Are they building your world up or tearing it down?

Are they creating a positive flow of energy in your life?

Thought and words are sometimes inseparable, spurring one another and can be building upon one another or corrupting one another. Or, as George Orwell so eloquently put it in his novel *1984*, "But if thought corrupts language, language can also corrupt thought."[23]

Remember, thought and words are intertwined, and even though the latter will originate in the former, together they have the power to create who and what we will become.

"If we condense our thoughts to focus on the words we are going to say and why we are saying them, then we can properly wield tremendous power over our lives."

So, think—for your mind, your thoughts are your most powerful tool. As the author and physician Oliver Wendell Holmes, Sr. has been quoted as saying, "Speak clearly, if you speak at all; carve every word before you let it fall."[24]

"Speak clearly, if you speak at all; carve every word before you let it fall."[1]

Oliver Wendell Holmes, Sr.

CHAPTER 3

WORDS

Deep in the woods, there were a group of frogs merrily hopping along and enjoying the beautiful sunshine. Being content to just hop in the warm sun, they were not watching where they were going. Then, two of the frogs unwittingly hopped into a deep pit. These two frogs fell hard, knocking the air out of themselves, and for a few moments they just lay still, on their backs, looking up. They saw the rest of the frogs in the group gather around the opening of the pit as they peered at the two in the hole. The group tried to determine if there was any way they could help. When the frogs looking down saw how deep this pit was, they became dismayed and immediately decided there was nothing that could be done to save their companions.

One of the frogs even shouted down into the pit, "There is nothing we can do! Your fate is sealed!"

Well, the two frogs in the pit were not going down without a fight; they began jumping with all their might. They jumped and jumped and jumped. The rest of the frogs saw their futile effort and began to also jump up and down while shouting phrases such as, "It's hopeless." "Just give up." "There is no way out!" They even shouted things like, "It was your fault for not being careful and responsible!"

The two frogs stuck in the pit continued to jump with every ounce of energy they had. After a few hours of this futile attempt to jump out of the pit, all while their companions kept shouting words of negativity and hopelessness, one of the frogs decided to finally take heed to the words his companions were saying and stopped. Discouraged, he just laid there, weary, accepting his destiny in this hopeless pit, and died. However, the other frog continued to jump with more effort and even more intensity. Eventually, he jumped so high that he made it out of the pit.

Astonished at his miraculous escape, the other frogs asked, "We told you it was impossible; there was no way out; you should just give up and die." "What made you ignore us?" "How did you do this?"

The victorious frog stared at them while they talked, and, reading their lips, he replied, "I'm deaf. All I could see was you hopping up and down, waving, and shouting, but I could not read what it was you were saying. I thought you were cheering us on and encouraging us to keep trying."[2]

One frog was inspired to success; the other frog was discouraged to death.

Perserverance or surrender, success or failure, rich or poor, life or death—you get to choose. These are all potential outcomes we can have during each season of life; and the outcome, just like it was for the frogs, will be heavily influenced by us—our thinking and our words. The more you fill yourself with negative words, the more negative your thinking will become, and doubt will grow; the more you fill yourself with positive words, the more positive your thinking will become, and faith will grow.

"The significant problems we face cannot be solved at the same level of thinking we were at when we created them."[3] When we change our thoughts, we can change our perspective. And it was the perceived kind words that inspired this frog to keep trying, to keep pushing against all odds, until he found success in saving his life. A negative word can destroy or even end the life of someone stuck in an emotional pit, but a kind word could raise their spirit to overcome anything.

Thoughts create, and words can either inspire or discourage. Why? Because words are a tool we use to communicate our thoughts to each other. As James C. Humes put it, "Words are the essence of communication."[4]

Irving J. Lee [October 27, 1909—May 23, 1955], a past speech communications professor at Northwestern University, stated the importance and power our words, a form of communication, have in our world, as quoted in Richard Lederer's book *The Miracle Of Language*: "Communication plays a tremendous role in human affairs. It serves as a means of cooperation and as a weapon of conflict. With it, people can solve problems, erecting the towering structures of science and poetry -- and talk themselves into insanity and social confusion."[5]

The words we choose to speak to ourselves, to others, and to the world around us are vessels of tremendous power, either discouraging life or inspiring success. Words, just like thoughts, have power over our lives and our world. They can help build fantastic, wealthy, and world-changing empires, or they can crumble nations.

If you are consistently speaking negatively about your situation, the season of life you are in, your life itself, where you live, or where you were born, then the negative seeds you are planting with your words will grow to be the poison of discouragement: weary and hopeless.

"A negative word can destroy or even end the life of someone stuck in an emotional pit, but a kind word could raise their spirit to overcome anything."

American novelist Nathaniel Hawthorne stated it well when he wrote, "Words: So innocent and powerless as they are, as standing in a dictionary, how potent for good and evil they become in the hands of one who knows how to combine them."[6]

It is said that life and death are in the tongue. In fact, for those who read it, the Bible mentions the word "tongue" 129 times and in 126 verses.

Proverbs 18:21 says, "The tongue has the power of life and death…"[7] So, if we hold the power of both death and life on our tongue, then why would we ever let death be spoken? Why are we not always speaking positively? Come to think of it: why does it sometimes seem difficult to speak positively, especially when we find ourselves in a storm of life? Well, we must first control our thoughts, which, according to scientific research, are on average eighty-percent negative. If we can control our thoughts, we can control our words. A negative thought creates a negative world discouraged by a negative word; a positive thought creates a positive world inspired by a positive word.

"The tongue has the power of life and death,"[8] and our thoughts either birth or abort that life. We hold the power to better our circumstances, to better our environment, and to better our lives and the lives of others with that small steering device in our mouth. "When we put bits into the mouths of horses to make them obey us, we can turn the whole animal. Or take ships as an example. Although they are so large and are driven by strong winds, they are steered by a very small rudder wherever the pilot wants to go. Likewise, the tongue is a small part of the body, but it makes great boasts. Consider what a great forest is set on fire by a small spark."[9]

Religious materials are not the only place to find that there is great power in the tongue, and neither is the Bible the only book that talks about controlling our tongue, nor is God the only author discussing the power of our words. The power held in our words to inspire ourselves and others is found nearly everywhere and in nearly every religious and non-religious work.

A previous Hollywood writer and author, Robert Greene, understood the power of the tongue and wrote in his book *The 48 Laws of Power* that, "… the human tongue is a beast that few can master. It strains constantly to break out of its cage, and if it is not tamed, it will run wild and cause you grief."[10]

"The soothing tongue is a tree of life, but a perverse tongue crushes the spirit."[11]

Words. Such a powerful and inspirational communication tool that when wielded correctly can help inspire a positive view and help create a positive world. When we allow words to roll off our tongue and successfully ride the wave, then they hold dominance, but if we keep these words in check and wipe out the negative ones, then we hold dominance.

There is a fable from a man named Aesop, believed to be a slave, storyteller, and fabulist who lived in Greece between 620 and 564 BC, that speaks well of choosing our words and holding our tongue. In this fable, a tortoise who was exceedingly lazy was forever cursed with a shell, or house, upon his back so he could always be at home and forever continue his laziness. After many years of watching the other animals—squirrels, rabbits, and birds—freely move about and see the world, the tortoise became sad and depressed. Eventually, he talked to two ducks, who agreed to help him not only see the world but see it from a completely different perspective. He was told to hold on to a stick with his mouth while the ducks held each end and flew him over the countryside. The ducks told him to keep his mouth shut or it would end badly for him. While in the air, a crow, seeing this bizarre sight, flew by and said, "This must be the king of the turtles." The tortoise foolishly opened his mouth and pridefully spoke, "Why certainly." He immediately fell to his demise.[12]

Just as good words can inspire and build, so can negative and foolish words discourage and destroy.

"A negative thought creates a negative world discouraged by a negative word; a positive thought creates a positive world inspired by a positive word."

"The lips of fools bring them strife, and their mouths invite a beating. The mouths of fools are their undoing, and their lips are a snare to their very lives."[13]

"Word" is defined as "a speech sound or series of speech sounds that symbolizes and communicates a meaning" and "a written or printed character or combination of characters representing a spoken word."[14] Words are a communication tool used to express our thoughts, and, just like any tool, the impact words have is greatly determined by how they are used and the intentions of the user.

The words that leave our tongue hold immense and, as some might say, unparalleled power. This power has the ability to bring nations to war or to bring freedom to millions.

So, what are you speaking into your life?

What are you speaking over other's lives?

Remember, words cost nothing to formulate and communicate; it's how we choose to use our words that could ultimately cost us.

As was mentioned previously about the bits in the mouths of horses, the tongue is our bit, controlling the environment around us and the world into which we walk. For better or for worse, our words are a powerful tool that helps control our path. We have the power to control those words by using our brain, our mind, to think before we speak, and in doing so, we help to better control and shape our world. "Everyone should be quick to listen, slow to speak and slow to become angry…"[15] Be quick to listen and think before you speak.

If we choose not to pause and think and our words are left unchecked, they can be like a death grip that holds still our ability to grow, leaving us breathless and ultimately squeezing the life out of us. Negative words have the astonishing ability to attach to and defile the unconscious, effectively obliterating one's own spirit and, like the frog, leaving them hopeless. Or, as the English poet Robert Southey wrote, "It is with words as with sunbeams—the more they are condensed, the deeper they burn."[16] Our words should be carefully considered before spoken.

I remember a very trying time for me when I was in college, and negativity began to overtake my thoughts and exit my mouth with words of discouragement and hopelessness. I was sitting at a computer wallowing in my newly constructed dungeon, trying to see beyond the darkness and focus on finishing an assignment, when the weight of my worrisome and negative thoughts became too much. I had been informed that due to some oversight, I would have to take extra classes and stay at least another year. For weeks, all I could think about was the extra time it would take me to graduate and the amount of debt I might have when finished. I was a little older than my classmates when I decided to finish my schooling. So, I was not a traditional student, and this reason probably had something to do with the extra time the school said would be required before I could obtain my degree.

Well, this constant negative thinking created enormous stress and an internal sense of depression—a depression I would keep alive by speaking these negative thoughts over myself every day. I would think and say things like, "You are so stupid for going into debt for an education," "You're never going to make enough to pay this back," "You're always going to be in debt because you were a fool," "I'm never going to finish school," "I'll never be able to chase my dreams with this load on my back," and "They added another year to my schooling; do I even know this field?"

My words were helping to hold me prisoner to the world I let my thinking of perceived worries and fears create, and this world began to grow dark, cloudy, and stormy, as was evident by the torrential rain that was breaking free from the dam known as the tear glands.

"Our words should be carefully considered before spoken."

It took a few weeks, but when I began changing my thinking and my speaking to be more positive, such as "This is only for a short time," "I'm supposed to be here," and "This will be a great thing for my life," my attitude and environment began to change for the better. I could begin to see a positive in what I thought was only a negative. "Consider what a great forest is set on fire by a small spark,"[17] because "From a little spark may burst a flame,"[18] and that flame will either be uncontrolled and burn the forest or contained and light your path and warm your soul.

One important thing I must tell you here is that although we, ultimately, hold the power to choose what we will think and speak, when we find ourselves in that deep pit, just like the frog that escaped, we will need and greatly benefit from the help of another. "At times our own light goes out and is rekindled by a spark from another person. Each of us has cause to think with deep gratitude of those who have lighted the flame within us."[19]

Well, I used that former perceived period of time of personal negativity and hopelessness to write a poem that, in the latter perceived period of time, I later turned into a short film, which was then nominated for an award at a film festival the next year. I had to make a choice to change my thinking to see the good and positive and change my speaking to the same. Then, and only then, could I begin to see the light, to see a positive, and to inspire myself so that I might regain that hope and joy for life.

As Charles R. Swindoll said, "Life is 10% what happens to you and 90% how you react to it."[20]

I believe there is an opportunity for good in everything; however, if our thoughts are too focused on negativity and we are too busy speaking negative words, then we will be like a person in quicksand, sinking further and further into our pit of despair when one positive branch, one positive word, could save us—if only we would open our mind to see it.

The words we speak have the power to inspire or discourage our place in life, to inspire or discourage how we perceive ourselves, to inspire or discourage how others perceive us, and, most importantly, to inspire or discourage who we become. So, if we are going to speak, let us speak positive words of inspiration, or at the very least, speak less.

Politicians effectively understand the power of the tongue and use it daily to persuade listeners to their benefit. Generals use the power of words to rally and encourage their troops. Jesus used the power of words to heal the sick and cast out demons. "… Two demon-possessed men coming from the tombs met him. They were so violent that no one could pass that way. The demons begged Jesus, 'If you drive us out, send us into the herd of pigs.' He [Jesus] said to them, 'Go!' So they came out and went into the pigs…"[21]

A man who was known for few words and was nicknamed "Silent Cal," President Calvin Coolidge, understood the value of words and thus chose them carefully, as described in this story: "A woman in a receiving line at the White House once gushed to him, 'Mr. President, I bet my husband that I could get you to say more than two words.' 'You lose,' was Coolidge's reply."[22]

Just because one can speak, speak loudly, or even speak often, it does not equate to one being positive or even wise. Confusingly, the same can be said for one who does not speak often: "Even fools are thought wise if they keep silent, and discerning if they hold their tongues."[23]

Yeah, but remember this old saying: Sticks and stones may break my bones, but words will never hurt me. So, actions speak louder than words, and words are cheap. Words are meaningless. Do you agree with this? It is true that "faith by itself, if it is not accompanied by action, is dead."[24] But does this mean that words are truly meaningless? It is something that has been said to me before, and it is something that I once thought was true. However, if this were true and words truly hold no power and no control, if words are truly meaningless, if words truly never hurt, if words truly never help heal, then how does a poem or a letter from a loved one affect us? And how come we are hurt by the words someone might speak to us, sometimes even devastated?

"So, if we are going to speak, let us speak positive words of inspiration, or at the very least, speak less."

Sammy Hagar correctly said, "Words have power. They work. That's why poetry can affect people. That's why music and lyrics and songs affect people, and that's why chants and prayers and affirmations and all those various things affect the frame of mind."[25] They do this by the meaning we attach to the communication tool that is our words, and we attach that meaning to our own thoughts. So, yes. Words do have power; words can and do affect our lives; there is power in the tongue.

The words we say inspire the formation of our path and help in the molding of us and the world around us.

It is not just religious teachings and believers that understand the power of words. Science has proven the power of words. One example I found very intriguing was Dr. Masaru Emoto's water experiment.[26] Dr. Emoto was a researcher, entrepreneur, author, and a doctor of alternative medicine. He believed that the physical structures of water could be changed through vibrations and what he considered "emotional energy." He truly believed that water was a blueprint of our reality and that words could alter that blueprint.

Throughout the 1990s, Dr. Emoto performed numerous experiments on water and had professional photographers take photographs of the water's structure at the end of each experiment. These experiments documented the physical effects words, prayer, music, and the environment had on the water and its crystalline structure—water crystals. Dr. Emoto said, "… we have come to the conclusion that the water is reacting to the actual words. For example, for our trip to Europe we tried using the words 'thank you' and 'you fool' in German. The people on our team who took the actual photographs of the water crystals did not understand the German for 'you fool,' and yet we were able to obtain exactly the same kind of results in the different crystal formations based on the words used."[27]

He also found that the water tested with positive, pleasing, and uplifting words formed far more symmetrical and aesthetically pleasing crystalline structures. Whether you agree with Dr. Emoto and his research and findings or not, the evidence of his water experiments is just one of many examples documenting and showcasing the power words hold.

The water crystal study is amazing to me because, if water structure can be shaped by positive words, music, and a good environment, then why can't we be similarly shaped? The human body, as most of us learned in our middle school science classes, is scientifically proven to be more than 60% water. Based on the water crystal experiment alone, this should inspire thought about the ability to change and inspire oneself and the world through the power of words, positive words.

Words can create; words can destroy; words can lift up; words can beat down; words can inspire or discourage; the tongue speaks love or it speaks hate; you speak death or you speak life. To succumb to temptation and speak ill is to be foolhardy and wounding, but to hold your tongue can show great control and wisdom, and to speak wisely can inspire another to greatness.

So, if words truly do hold such power over the structure of our lives, then why must we continually refresh our minds with positive thinking and speak positively all the day? Why not just speak good one day, let that positivity inspire our world to take shape, and then be done with it?

If only it were that simple, but, alas, life requires more effort; it requires a continuous flow to keep the momentum and move us through the white-water rapids of life.

Much like the Bible states in Joshua 1:8

"... meditate on it day and night ..."[28] so does Dr. Emoto explain why these water crystal structures do not last forever: "We refer to the crystalline structure of water as 'clusters.' The smaller the clusters, the longer the water will retain its memory. If there is too much space between the clusters, other information could easily infiltrate this space, making it hard for the clusters to hold the integrity of the information...A tight bonding structure is best for maintaining the integrity of information."[29]

By meditating, or thinking, on good, positive and uplifting thoughts and saying good, uplifting and positive words every day, we are essentially ensuring that the "clusters" of our life hold together and continually build toward our better future. These clusters, when held together, act as our raft, keeping us afloat on life's rapids; without them we would surely drown in our own negativity and misery.

As the old saying goes, "you reap what you sow." A farmer doesn't sow in only one season, one time, and reap a positive and plentiful crop every year after; he must sow each season for there to be a crop each year. So too must we continually sow seeds of good and positivity in our own lives through our thoughts and words if we want to reap good and positivity: "… whatever is true, whatever is noble, whatever is right, whatever is pure, whatever is lovely, whatever is admirable—if anything is excellent or praiseworthy—think about such things."[30]

> *"The words we say inspire the formation of our path and help in the molding of us and the world around us."*

Our response comes from our thoughts; a prideful and foolish thought communicated through words could destroy a life, but a modest and kind thought communicated through words could save a life.

Who am I to make a change,

Or break away and rearrange.

Rank and file for all my days.

Depart the negative, there is no way.

Surly this path, it is my fate.

Inmost part of my being

Necessitate the drive to free me,

Show me how I can change thee.

Provide reprieve and bring back meaning.

Inspire me, help me believe.

Reshape my mind to positivity;

Every thought create the world in me.

Unwrap the gift of creativity

So I may inspire others like me.[31]

When a person is emotionally struggling, one word could change their world. As Colin Cherry, who was a British cognitive scientist and a communication pioneer, said in his book *On Human Communication*, "Words can arouse every emotion: awe, hate, terror, nostalgia, grief... Words can demoralize a person into torpor, or they can spring a person into delight; they can raise him to heights of spiritual and aesthetic experience. Words have frightening power."[32]

Words are like a powerful spell that, when spoken, has the power to grip the heart and mind of someone and, with one word in one instant, magically shift their attention, their focus, and their emotions from good to bad, happy to sad, peace to strife, or death to life.

As Irving J. Lee said, "Verbal communication from the earliest infantile dependence of the child on his parents to the developed uses of the full citizenship, scientific speech and words of command and leadership, is the correlate of this. The knowledge of right words, appropriate phrases and the more highly developed forms of speech, gives man a power over and above his own limited field of personal action. But this power of words, this co-operative use of speech is and must be correlated with the conviction that a spoken word is sacred. The fact also that words add to the power of man over and above their strictly pragmatic effectiveness must be correlated with the belief that words have a mystical influence ... "[33]

So, what words are you choosing to speak into your life?

What words are you choosing to speak into the life of another?

Are your words building upon each other, laying a foundation of positivity, and inspiring your life and others to build a better world and to pave a better destiny?

Are you living an inspired life or a discouraged life?

I would like to leave you with this prayer. I am unaware of who it was originally attributed to, but I feel it speaks truth nonetheless.

"Lord, make my words as sweet as honey, for tomorrow I may have to eat them."[34]

"Every thought you produce, anything you say, any action you do, it bears your signature."[1]

Thich Nhat Hanh

CHAPTER 4

ACTIONS

Captain Chris was a prominent sailor of the high seas in the early 1700's. He captained a crew of fifteen men on a ship measuring about one hundred feet in length and twenty-five feet in width—a small ship for the size of the crew and the nature of his business. For you see, Captain Chris was a famed pirate. He and his crew were known throughout the seas as "the crew that moves," not only for their restless nature but also for their success in being able to persuade merchants and other sailors.

Captain Chris and his crew would constantly

sail the seas, back and forth, searching for wayward ships and vessels loaded with treasure and the most luxurious product known to his ragtag assemblage of pirates—rum. When they spotted a vessel to raid, Captain Chris would think about his possibilities of a successful attack, then he would give an inspiring speech to his crew to rally them for battle. Then he and his crew would take action: they would fly their unique pirate flag and then sail toward their goal. Captain Chris would do one other thing that no other pirate did at that time: he would shout to his would-be plundered acquisition and communicate to those who dared fight back what he and his crew were about to do. The crew would be taking the treasures and goods on board and would kill anyone who stood in their way. However, he would also inform them that if they abandoned their vessel and left the majority of their goods, they would be spared, and they could take enough supplies to sustain themselves on their trip, in their lifeboats, to the nearest island; this was a kind-hearted gesture by one of the most feared and successful pirates on the high seas.

Well, one day they sailed upon the port (left) side of a British ship in the distance. Captain Chris took out his spyglass and searched the ship from bow to stern and back again. He saw fast-moving figures, each carrying a small bag, and running about the deck. He noticed, after what seemed to be panicked running as if to fix a major leak or escape a burning construct with only enough time to save the meager belongings one could hold in their arms, that each figure turned toward the starboard (right) side and disappeared. He watched for several minutes, trying to catch a glimpse of any figure reappearing again, but none did. After what felt like an eternity to his crew, who were now rubbing their hands together and licking their lips in anticipation of the treasures and possibility of rum on this ship they were watching from afar, Captain Chris gave the order to sail toward the soon-to-be conquered goods.

As they approached, they noticed that the ship, which appeared to be moving forward with forward momentum and steering in a straight line toward an unknown destination, was now floating aimlessly and that there was no movement on deck. Captain Chris, approaching cautiously at this new sight, made his normal speech. No reply. He and his crew then boarded the vessel, with Captain Chris boarding first, and they began the search for their treasures and any sign of life. They found their treasure, but there was no life on board. Then, they noticed the lifeboats were missing on the starboard side.

After a couple of minutes, Captain Chris was called into the captain's quarters by one of his men, who had found a note hastily written on the captain's desk. The note read:

"Captain Chris, we saw your ship and though we tried to outrun you we realized it was futile. We were ordered by our employer not to lose this cargo or else we face the gallows—a gesture our employer seems to love.

Knowing we face death in either scenario, but knowing you are a man of your word (your actions line up with what you say), we took the liberty to abandon this ship and start a new life on a nearby island with our precious belongings."

This became the norm of many successful plunders for Captain Chris, where no sailor was seen when boarded, and no blood was spilled.

Just as Captain Chris's words inspired his men to action and his actions of going into battle alongside his men moved them into battle, his actions toward those whom he was about to conquer (that of letting them leave peacefully and with supplies; hope for survival) led others to move toward trusting him at his word. Captain Chris walked the walk.

Let us not forget the immense power in words to inspire people and generations. Great revolutions took place because of the power of words to inspire the people into action. Remember it was thoughts put into words that communicated to the masses and inspired and sparked every type of revolution. Without thought and without words, there would quite possibly be no action.

We have already discussed how powerful words can be. Words can be uplifting, motivational, and inspiring; in fact, that is what words used properly can do: inspire. However, without action to back them up, words can appear hollow, void, and even hypocritical.

As Mark Twain is attributed with stating, "actions speak louder than words..."[2] This is a powerful statement. Why is that? If words inspire, if words are powerful enough to hold the power of life and death, then why would actions speak louder than words? Well, the answer is a simple one: **Actions move**.

We could just sit and think and speak good things all day long, but in our thoughts, we create that positivity; in our words, we inspire that positivity, and just as "faith by itself, if it is not accompanied by action, is dead,"[3] action is required to move.

As humans, we tend to believe what is tangible, what we can see; without seeing it, it is usually assumed to be fictional or a faith belief. It is the words in a speech that inspire crowds and energize people for a cause, but without the proper actions following and supporting the words spoken, people would not continue to move. The inspiration from words is great, but it is fleeting—that is why people read devotionals, speak affirmations, and tune in regularly to motivational speakers every day to stay inspired and motivated. It is the action that keeps people rallied to, well, action. When action lines up with words, action is powerful.

"Let us not forget the immense power in words to inspire people and generations."

Before World War II, it was words that

inspired the German people to rise up behind Adolf Hitler. His profound speeches inspired millions to rally behind him and propel his ideas, his desires, and his agenda. If it were not for the power of words, he might not have had the chance to later implement his actions of atrocities of which he so deeply desired. The words he spoke shook people's emotions and brought inspiration to their troubled lives. The words he spoke brought the masses together and inspired the German people. The words he spoke shook the foundation of the political culture; he made some statements that, although they were not the truth, were still true and inspired the revolutionary base to take violent actions of oppression. His words held great power of inspiration and motivation, yet it was his actions—genocide, leading the Germans to death and defeat through his own personal hatred and pride, murder, and hypocritical actions that deviated from his words—that moved the world, and even other Germans, including some German generals, to fight against him and Nazism. It was his actions that caused Valkyrie to take place: a mass coup by some high-level German officials to assassinate Hitler and end the war to save Germany. Some of these people, such as general Erwin Rommel, were supporters of Hitler and his vision to "save Germany and its people" from the very beginning, based on his words and speeches, yet they eventually changed sides and tried to end Hitler's life and the devastating war because of his actions.

Think about how much "good" and "inspiration" and "motivation" are spoken by politicians and other individuals—speeches of hope, unity, and love—that rally those who hear to emotional highs of inspiration and motivation toward the politician's own personal or selfish goal. The power of their words inspires others to join them and motivates them to support them. They cheer and chant, they give donations, and they praise the individual based upon a speech and the words they communicate with, usually without much thought to the individual's actual character, record, or deeds—their true and actual actions.

What happens, though, when their actions say otherwise? From small actions to large actions, there should be no difference if the action does not line up with the words spoken. Two examples are (they were not chosen for any political reason but for their popularity and position in history) former American President Barack Hussein Obama and (at the time of the first edition of this writing) American President Donald John Trump. There were many examples we could choose for each, and a plethora of examples we could have chosen before and since these two were in office, but I decided to use a well-known and publicized one to represent a large action and a little-known and often ignored one to represent a small action.

In what some might claim is a small white lie in terms of words but hypocritical and wrong in terms of actions not lining up with words,

Obama stated in 2008 that "...there are legitimate concerns in not wanting to allow people to grow their own [marijuana] or start setting up mom-and-pop shops, because... it becomes fairly difficult to regulate... I'm not going to be using Justice Department resources to try to circumvent state laws on the issue..."[4] Yet he ended up exceeding even former American President George Bush's aggressiveness on marijuana. As stated in multiple news sites and articles, such as the 2012 Mother Jones magazine article, "The president campaigned on the promise that he'd stop federal raids on medical marijuana operations that were in compliance with state laws ... but then ... raided more than 100 dispensaries in its first three years ..."[5] His words comforted some and inspired others to continue their path of small business in the area of medical marijuana, but his actions sent a different message and moved some to distrust him.

"The power of their words inspires others to join them and motivates them to support them."

President Donald Trump made a promise that he would build a wall on the southern border and that the wall would be paid for by Mexico. In 2015, then as a presidential candidate, Trump stated, "I will build a ... wall on our southern border. And I will have Mexico pay for that wall."[6] This statement would lead one to believe that Mexico would not just pay for the wall, be it through a span of time or by paying the United States back the money spent at a later date, but pay for it from the beginning of construction. His actions, however, have stated otherwise. Almost four years after saying those words that inspired some, he took action as President that was contrary to his word and would require American citizens, not just Mexicans, to help pay for the wall. His words comforted some and inspired others with the hope of further security at no additional cost to them, but his actions sent a different message and moved some to distrust him.

Those are just two small examples of words inspiring people, in this case to help gain support or votes for a specific person, but the person's actions not lining up with the words spoken, leading some to oppose and criticize the original orator of those words. As one person put it, "Your negative actions will always speak over top of your kind words and only fools listen where the wise watch."[7] We must be careful what we promise with the words we speak, for the inspiration will require proper action.

Actions move.

The question is, in which direction are your actions moving you and those watching you?

So, what exactly is action then? Action is defined as "a thing done," "an act of will," and the "process of doing something."[8] Action is movement. If one only thinks or talks but never moves, then there is no action.

Thoughts create. Words inspire. Actions move.

You choose what thoughts to create; you choose which words to speak; and you choose the actions you take.

When you speak inspiration into someone's life, will your actions move them along with you in the direction of your inspiring words, or will your actions be hypocritical and move them to oppose you?

Sometimes the words we hear may not line up with the actions taken, but I truly believe, and I suspect it must be the case to explain their true intentions to move those helping in secret, that they have spoken those words to others, which line up perfectly with their terrible and bad actions. The moment we hear an inspirational and uplifting speech is a mere blip in the amount of words spoken in private about the true intentions, about the true actions to be taken, if those true intentions and the actions taken move in the opposite direction of that mere blip in time.

If the words spoken are disingenuous when compared to the actions taken, then the actions taken must be compared with the thoughts of the original orator of the disingenuous words spoken. I think Marcus Aurelius understood the importance of actions with his quote, "Let it be your constant method to look into the design of people's actions and see what they would be at, as often as it is practicable; and to make this custom the more significant, practice it first upon yourself."[9]

"Action is movement. If one only thinks or talks but never moves, then there is no action."

Pay attention to people's actions if you wish to know where they are headed. Pay attention to your own actions if you wish to understand your current path to destiny.

Actions follow words, and words follow thought.

From our thoughts, we create our destiny; in our words, we inspire or discourage our destiny; and the path of our actions moves us toward that destiny.

As Henri Bergson accurately put it, "Think like a man of action, and act like a man of thought."[10]

Many years ago, when I was still a teenager, I would spend countless hours in the gym—not weightlifting but running and practicing my skills at the game of basketball. Not to brag, but I was pretty good back in the day. I could shoot three-pointers with the best of them, and I would often lead my team in rebounds and steals.

Dribbling the ball was another thing, however; I wasn't bad, but I was no point guard—I was always a forward or center. Anyway. There was even one year I led the league in rebounds. I know, I used to pat myself on the back for my awesome skills because, at that time, I wrongly believed skills made the man. However, these skills meant nothing after a moment of lapse in judgment; well, that moment was being built throughout the game and some time before.

It was a pickup game, full court, five-on-five. My mindset at that time was to win; if our team won, then we stayed on the court; if not, then we got back in line and hoped we could play another game that day. Well, my mind was not just set on the positivity of my ability to play but, more importantly, it was set on winning—winning was all that mattered. With that, I was thinking of myself rather than others—when we are focused on ourselves, the ends tend to justify the means, and when the ends justify the means, the mean is us.

On one play, the other team passed the ball down court, and I reached out to steal the pass. My fingers grazed the ball, and the ball went out of bounds. The referee, either by placement or momentary lapse of attention (I'm still not sure which), said he did not see if I touched the ball or not, and he directly asked me if I had touched it. Since the game was close and this was near the end, I said no; I wanted the ball, and I wanted victory. A player on the other team heard my answer and argued with me and the ref about it. I was adamant that I did not touch the basketball before it went out of bounds, but it was clear, if one was watching, that I did touch the ball. The referee said he did not see it and that the final answer to this argument was left up to me. I walked to the edge of the court, took the ball, and said they touched it last and that it was our ball. A bald-faced lie backed with a brazen action based on a thought pattern formed on self and justified by the ends.

Oh, and that game I so desperately wanted

to win that I was willing to be self-centered, mean, sell out my character, and lie about it, yeah, we lost.

As bad as it can be to not have actions line up with words, it is still much more powerful and long lasting when the actions do line up with the words. Actions that line up with the words spoken can become a rarity in this world. That is why when it happens those who live it are revered, they are remembered through time.

Take Jesus of Nazareth as an example. Here is a name and story that I am sure most people have heard of. According to the Bible, Jesus spoke words of love, servanthood, and faith. In Matthew 5:47, Jesus said, "And if you greet only your own people, what are you doing more than others? Do not even pagans do that?"[11] Love those who do you wrong; love those who disagree with you; love your enemies.

If you only love those who are like you and who agree with you, then what are you doing differently than the rest of the world?

What are you doing differently than everyone else?

Remember, though, that love is not just acceptance and participation; it also teaches, rebukes, corrects, and trains. And love in correction brings learning.

> *"Pay attention to your own actions if you wish to understand your current path to destiny."*

Jesus spent time in prayer, working on his thoughts and making sure they lined up with the Word of God. Then, when his thoughts were positive, good, and uplifting, he spoke those creative thoughts into inspirational words, which we know as wisdoms, parables, and stories. Then he did something that few of us can do each and every day: He walked the walk. Jesus' actions followed those of his teachings. His actions lined up with the words he spoke. Jesus ate with the wealthy, the poor, the religious, the non-religious, believers, and sinners. He talked with, helped, and uplifted Jews, Gentiles, Pharisees, prostitutes, thieves, believers, and non-believers. He did not let his teachings or his beliefs hinder him from helping and loving those who believed differently than him. He did not falter in his belief, his faith, or his path, and he did not compromise, trade, violate, or alter His values, character, or any part of God's Word, but he reached out, with tolerance and love, to those who did not believe the same and to those who called for his death. He did not necessarily participate in the very activities of sinners or condone what his enemies were doing. Besides, without an absolute, how can anyone truly know what is truth or moral, and how can anyone truly know what is "love"? He corrected and taught them, and He even rebuked them at times with the truth in love. He thought and meditated on love, He talked about love, and He acted on love. This is one reason we still speak of Jesus, even today. Those who do not believe in God or the Bible even invoke his name to this day: "What would Jesus do?" "You're not very Christian-like," and "Jesus wouldn't do that." Do what? Jesus would not allow his thoughts to deviate from what was creatively good, his words to deviate from his inspirationally positive message, or his actions to move in any direction other than the inspiration of his words and the creation of his positive thoughts.

How many of us can say our daily actions always line up with our words? How about half of our daily actions?

Our actions, even our silent actions such as a wave or a smile, can sometimes convey more than words ever could. Our actions can give the world a clear signal to the type of world our thoughts are forming and the type of person our thoughts are creating; a hand on the shoulder of a grieving neighbor, the sneer on a lip when speaking of unity, the charge into battle when speaking of bravery, the serving of others without a demand for a return.

Thoughts come before words, words come before action, and action moves.

I act as I think,

I think I will bloom like spring;

Beauty brought to life.[12]

So, what is it that you are acting upon?

Are your actions helping others?

Are your actions helping create a better world and a better you?

Are your actions following positive thinking?

Are your actions moving yourself and others to a better future, a better destiny?

Author and public speaker Rob Bell said it well when he wrote, "What we do comes out of who we believe we are."[13] Who we believe we are is formed in our thoughts, and we will inevitably act as the person we have created in our thoughts. As Marcus Aurelius put it, "The soul becomes dyed with the color of its thoughts."[14]

Actions that line up with the spoken path are powerful, loud, and moving, but it still requires words to keep the movement going through continual inspiration. Or to finish Mark Twain's statement from earlier in this chapter, "Actions speak louder than words, but not nearly as often."[15]

"Humans are creatures of habit. If you quit when things get tough, it gets that much easier to quit the next time. On the other hand, if you force yourself to push through it, the grit begins to grow in you."[1]

Travis Bradberry

CHAPTER 5

HABITS

J udy is an unpredictable, strong, ferocious, and independent force that can disrupt and destroy without warning, but she is also very beautiful and a wonderful caregiver in her temperate state. Judy is Mother Nature personified.

One day, Judy was whistling through the trees as she gracefully led the tall grasses of the great plains in a hypnotic and rhythmic dance. She was relishing in the happiness she was bringing to the creatures of the earth: the plants, trees, birds, land animals, and all living things. The sunshine was bright, and the rays that fell brought warmth like that of putting on a freshly dried shirt right from the dryer. The wind was light and cooling, the flowers were blooming, and the smell of spring was in the air. All was calm and good.

Then, Judy heard faint voices from the edge of the tree line. These voices were boasting of growing so high, so strong, so independent, and so powerful that not even Mother Nature could move them. This intrigued and slightly infuriated Judy.

She thought, *Who could withstand me? What force could possibly grow another to a point of strength that the impossible could become possible? I must check this out.*

With that, Judy moved toward the voices.

When she arrived, she saw two young saplings and two adults rooting around. Camellia and Holly, the mature ones, were showing off their height and beauty to the two saplings, who looked up at them in awe.

Holly boasted, "I have roots, but I do not

like to be tied down, so I do not create a habit of them. I do not commit myself to any habit; this way, I can easily move wherever and whenever from one option to another. I can grow so tall that I can reach the sky, and, given enough time, I tend to grow on others."

"I want to be like you when I grow and not create a habit so I can easily be moved from one foundation to another too," said one of the saplings.

"Yeah," said the other sapling, "I don't know what I want yet, but I know I don't want to be tied down, so like you, I don't want deep roots, maybe no roots at all, so I can see where the wind takes me."

Then Leonard, a big oak of a being, interrupted and spoke slowly so the saplings would hopefully understand him and heed his words of wisdom.

With a deep voice, he said, "Good roots give you life; they give you strength; they give you identity; and, more importantly, they help you develop a strong character. It is not your height, beauty, or ability to just go with the wind that will strengthen you or even sustain you against the mighty forces of life. This, the habit of roots, is what will truly strengthen you against even Mother Nature."

Judy, no longer intrigued, became furious with another for questioning her power and ability and said to herself, "I will teach them that no force is powerful enough to stand against me, for I am Mother Nature. I am life."

She decided to blow a mighty wind at the defiant voices. She blew and blew, each breath more powerful than the previous. The two saplings, whose roots were not yet developed, were easily uprooted and gone the way of the wind, not to be seen again. Next were Camellia and Holly. These two were a little tougher because their roots were naturally grounded, but they were not habitually secured, so with a little effort they were still easy enough for Judy to uproot and blow away just like the saplings.

Leonard, however, stood his ground. No matter how strong a wind Judy blew at Leonard, he did not budge; he swayed with the wind but, ultimately, he held his ground. His roots were developed over a long period of time and habitually grew deep in the ground and held strong, holding him firmly in place against even the mighty force of Mother Nature.

Just as Leonard's roots were strong and powerful, so are good habits that are developed over time.

A good habit is a lifeline to the person we want to be and the life we wish to live. A bad habit is like a hole in a lifeboat; no matter how much or how hard we work to scoop the water out of our lifeboat, the bad habit will inevitably cause us to sink. We must work to plug that hole, to fix the bad habit by creating a new and better habit, in order to stay afloat and reach our goal.

This makes me think of a quote I read,

which ties in well with the root of these five traits, from which we can begin to uproot a bad habit and plant, grow, and, over time, secure the roots of a good habit—our thoughts. "You've been criticizing yourself for years, and it hasn't worked. Try approving of yourself and see what happens."[2] Why not? As the old saying goes, "If you want something different, then you must do something different." Create a good and better habit. Why? Because **habits form.**

Habit. This one thing is such a powerful and controlling force in our lives. Habits are said to be thousands of times stronger than our desires, and desires can be a strong motivating and inspiring force. This, I think, helps explain why it can be so frustratingly difficult for us to stick to and accomplish our New Year's resolutions: we desire a change, but our habits, unless changed, lead us back to our "normal" routine and away from the new goal of the resolution.

So why is it so frustrating and hard to change

a habit? Time, effort, and consciousness are the top answers that come to mind. According to a *European Journal of Social Psychology* research article published in 2010, the average time for a habit to stick is said to be about 66 days.[3] So, on average, it takes at least two months of dutiful, diligent, consistent, and conscious work to create a new habit; sometimes it might take a lot longer, but if you are conscious, diligent, and persistent, then you can create and initiate a new, better habit in and for your life. Repetitiousness, repetitive willful thought— here we are back at the root once again. It cannot be expected that a new habit would be created out of motivation or desire alone; these are temporary and based on feelings. It takes conscious effort, commitment, and a lot of patience for a new habit to be formed.

So, what exactly is a habit, then?

According to Merriam-Webster, a habit is "an acquired mode of behavior that has become nearly or completely involuntary," "a behavior pattern acquired by frequent repetition," and "the prevailing disposition or character of a person's thoughts and feelings."[4]

"A good habit is a lifeline to the person we want to be and the life we wish to live."

Feelings, much like motivation and desire, are temporary. Our feelings tend to change from moment to moment and are heavily dictated by our circumstances. Circumstances are nearly out of our control. However, we do control what we choose to think about; we choose the words we speak; we choose the actions we take; and we choose the habits we form. We choose how we will think about, speak to, and react to the circumstances. Therefore, we are not dictated by our circumstances, meaning we are not dictated by our feelings. You are more than just how you feel today or how a stranger might see you, and you are more than a statistic because you get to choose—you get to choose your destiny.

So, as I interpret it, habits are what our actions will lead us to do, unconsciously and without provocation. They stem from our repeated thoughts which are manifested into spoken word and manipulated by our action and, now, unconsciously driving our daily life. Habit is ingrained in us through repetition and habitually paves our outcome. A habit, as I think about it, is an acronym, which means you "Have Ability By Initiating Thought."

In short, a habit is a behavior created through repetition and unconsciously executed. Our behavior is our response to our environment; it is a response to stimulation; it is "the way in which someone conducts oneself."[5] Behavior is the fruit of our habits, which are the stems of our repeated actions, which are the branches of the words we choose to speak, which is the trunk of the thoughts we allow to take root and be implanted in and of our life.

Repetition is a process, and this process is what leads to habits. We think of something, we say something, we do something, then we repeat; eventually, this process will ingrain this habit in our unconscious, and we will say those words or perform those actions almost every time and without conscious thought in those situations and in our daily lives.

Hold on! What was all that? I know, I sometimes miss the correction of my habit of the old, repeated adage, "Say what it is you are going to say, then say it, then remind people of what you said." Though this usually works well for the remembrance of a point, there are times it can overload the senses or even become confusing. Yet, confusion can sometimes be good. As Larry Leissner stated, "If confusion leads to knowledge, then I must be a genius."[6] Hey, it is the confusion that typically leads me to do a lot of research, and, usually, it grows my understanding.

So, in the hope of clearing up any confusion,

here is a fun way to think about it (well, maybe not fun, but when I thought of it, I thought it was funny): "Rabit": Repetition breeds habit.

Habit is an almost involuntary, unconscious pattern of action or speech (a behavior) that encompasses our daily lives. Behavior is the way we conduct ourselves because of our habits. Our behavior is what most people use to put a label on our identity, which is based on our character. And all this comes from the root, which is our thought.

The thoughts we think create, the words we speak inspire, the actions we take move, and the habits we conduct form. They form our behavior, which reflects on our identity and greatly helps shape our character.

"Habit is ingrained in us through repetition and habitually paves our outcome."

So, what are you forming as a habit?

What behaviors are your habits creating in you?

Our thoughts breed like "rabits." Did you see what I did there? "Rabit" (R-A-B-I-T): Repetition breeds habit. Our thoughts create the words of inspiration or discouragement we speak and the actions that move us to the habits we form.

What are you thinking about, saying, and doing over and over again without fail and most likely without conscious thought? Is it something good, something that will help you achieve your goals or create the person you want to be and the world you want to live in?

Are you forming habits that will reflect well on your destiny?

I'll tell you about one of my habits that cost me years of my working life. However, when I say cost me it's because everything costs something, but not every cost is beneficial in reaching a destiny of life; but as long as we learned from it and choose to change, then the cost was not a waste. Anyway. At the time, and even for a short while after, I wallowed in my self-pity for the years that I felt were flushed down the drain. My apathy for life grew and grew; it became so intense that once again I lost sight of even the faintest light of hope.

"Hope is being able to see that there is light despite all of the darkness."[7] Hope is one of the most important things, or gifts, for us; it is the vision for a better tomorrow; it helps give us strength in adversity and the willpower to persevere. And it is willpower, because, like we mentioned in the beginning: we make. The other two, in case you were wondering, are faith and love. Faith is complete trust; hope is a confident expectation or anticipation that is built on faith because hope is something that is not yet. "But hope that is seen is no hope at all. Who hopes for what they already have?"[8] Hope involves something not yet seen except in the mind's eye. Therefore, what you choose to allow to enter your thoughts and consequently keep rehearsing, you choose to create; for what you choose to create, you are choosing to have faith in, to trust in; and when you choose to have faith in the bad and negative, if that is what you are rehearsing and creating in your mind, then your hope will soon follow—it will become dark, gloomy, depressing, and soon it will be extinguished. This is just another reason why it is so important to take control of what you allow to enter your mind and think about, meditate on, rehearse, and become a habit of thought, for this will become the inspiration or discouragement in the words you speak, and it will be the actions that move you toward the path of life or death, and it will become the habits that will form your character and your destiny.

During this period of time, my thinking became a foggy wasteland blurred by the smoke from my burning dreams, which were doused in self-doubt, fear, stress, confusion, and the most pestilent and flammable of all thoughts, negativity. All of this led to a negative perception of life and self-worth.

Honestly, this is something that I have learned way too many people battle with, and it is something that has reared its ugly head in my life many times—negative thinking and low self-worth.

Well, in the season of negativity for this story, I was asked by the head of a certain department to come work for them, and, wanting a change from where I was, I said yes. Along with my transfer, I was promised opportunities for raises, promotions, and training so that I might be able to fully work in this new career field.

For the first couple of years, I learned all I could, and I even trained others who were placed over me. Then the day finally came to interview for and accept the next position. I had been trained for this position by the previous employee, and I knew this position inside and out. Then, the first sign of this bad habit was born when I was not offered the job. Time went by, and so did other people advancing, but I remained still. For more than a decade I worked for this department, learning, growing, and becoming, according to their words, the best in that position. And yet, almost nothing: little to no raises, no extra training, no advancement, no moving up the ladder, even ignored for awards for years of service at the ceremonies. As this was going on, I planted seeds that should never have been allowed, and I continued to nourish a fruitless tree buried deep in the wasteland of my negative and selfish thoughts. These thoughts became a daily habit of my thinking, and soon my words followed. It was not long after that my actions followed my words: I did less and less at work, and I stopped even trying to learn anything new at the job. Like I said before, feelings are temporary. Our feelings change from moment to moment and are heavily dictated by our circumstances. Circumstances are nearly out of our control. Such as: in my perception, those in charge refused to honor any of the promises made, and I was overlooked and undervalued, and this negativity in my mind caused me to "feel" used, worthless, talentless, stupid, and resentful. However, we do control what we choose to think, speak, and how we will act. I was wrongly and foolishly allowing the circumstances and others around me to influence my worth, attitude, and identity. As the saying goes, "you reap what you sow," and what I sowed was negativity into the soil of my foundation, which poisoned the soil and began to kill the roots of life in my mind; I foolishly chose to rehearse and nurture the creation of the bad and negativity.

Thoughts of *"You have no skill, no ability, no worth." "Why even try?" "What's the point?" "I might as well do something else while I'm here"* and others continuously ran through my mind, day in and day out. All lies, but sometimes lies feel more comforting than the truth when we are in a valley. Why? Because the truth often hurts our egos, our pride, and our feelings of entitlement, and because it often requires work, the truth sometimes hurts. Well, I manifested the habit of laziness, of self-doubt in all areas, of the woe is me mindset, and began torturing myself and crippling any good destiny I might reach with the habit, really it should be called selfishness and a self-centered mindset, of entitlement thinking.

"I should have that position," "I should get the pay raise," "I should be in charge," and *"I should…" "I deserve…" "I'm entitled…"* and *"I. I. I."* thoughts of victimhood and ingratitude ran through my head, and I even spoke these words many, many times. My actions even lined up with these bad habits of thought as the phrases "It's not my job, it's not my problem, let someone else deal with it" and "They screwed me, so screw them" became my mantra and apathy became my idol.

Honestly, these feelings resurfaced with each department I worked in while in this organization, even though I became the top person in the position I held in each department. Why would I stay at a place that I felt showed the same patterns of promises made and promises broken? Misplaced hope? The old adage says that comfort breeds complacency. Ignorance, maybe? I think those are all correct, but the biggest culprit, though, was fear—fear that if I went somewhere else, I would have to start all over, from the bottom up, and all these years (more than a decade) would be wasted; and I was getting older, so starting again was becoming even more frightening: I didn't have my whole working life to build something anymore; I only had half of it left, and I don't have the time to start over and to start with nothing. I thought, and sometimes still fight this, *"If I start over, I will not have enough to retire or take care of myself or a family, and how would I reconcile with those wasted years of my life?"* At least, that is the lie I found myself repeating in my mind.

The biggest problem with this habit of self-pity, laziness, disrespect, and selfish entitlement was that I stopped contributing to the business, and I stopped contributing and living my own life; I stopped working toward my dreams and toward the person I wanted to be. I stopped learning and growing, and, worst of all, I stopped serving. I no longer truly celebrated with others when good things happened for them at work. And as I said in the acknowledgments, "…when we are grateful for others, our focus shifts from selfish thoughts to thoughts of servitude." Well, I also missed opportunities outside of the job to learn and grow and reach a good and better destiny. Granted, I can now look back at this time in my life and learn from it, hopefully never repeating that path. I can also understand now why, as time went on, I was denied certain opportunities and reflect back on my thoughts, words, actions, and habits that, over time, portrayed an employee, a person, that was not completely faithful in the areas required and was not authentic.

It does not matter who broke what promise; we still have the choice to think, speak, act, and behave in a way that will form our path and reflect back on us. But if not for those times and the ability to reflect on and learn from the past, I would not have had, or even currently have, the opportunity to learn, grow, and build the habits that are leading me to become the man of character I want to be and to reach the good destiny. In fact, if I did not learn and change the path I found myself on, I would not have even thought about writing this book to help others. As they say, hindsight is 20/20.

Besides, something I have heard, learned, and still try to encourage myself with when the valleys in this journey of life appear and things "feel" dark, overwhelming, and gloomy is this: the season of life you are in today is only temporary; so why focus so much on the negativity and the storm, which are also temporary, when you have so many more spring days ahead?

Oh, that paver that engrains itself so deep that we involuntarily allow it to form our yellow brick road, which we unconsciously and merrily skip along without needing courage, heart, or a brain to reach its destiny. Thinking of it this way, it would seem we are at the mercy of our habits. Why is that?

"Are you forming habits that will reflect well on your destiny?"

According to Charles Duhigg in his book *The Power of Habit: Why We Do What We Do in Life and Business*, "When a habit emerges, the brain stops fully participating in decision making. It stops working so hard, or diverts focus to other tasks. So unless you deliberately fight a habit…the pattern will unfold automatically."[9] The reason for something like this, according to neuroscientist Elliot Berkman, is because "longtime habits are literally entrenched at the neural level, so they are powerful determinants of behavior." Like what was mentioned earlier, habits are ingrained in us over a period of time and become a part of our behavior through a process of repetition—or, in some rare cases, through a traumatic incident. This is why desire and motivation are not enough by themselves to change a habit or behavior because they are temporary feelings of conscious thought. This is also why, as Berkman states, "[it is] much easier to start doing something new than to stop doing something habitual without a replacement behaviour."[10]

When we start doing something new, we are using our conscious mind to think about the new task and, if repeated enough and for enough time, the new habit. We create the new behavior in our mind and deliberately focus on performing it. When doing this, we tend to believe we are in charge of our habits, but the reality is that the moment we cease to think about the new task or action (if we have not given the effort and time for it to stick with us), we will inevitably fall back into the routine of the old habit. Did you catch that? The moment we cease to think, because our thoughts create. If we stop thinking and have not given the effort and time for this new thought, this new habit to stick, our unconscious mind kicks in, and we unknowingly perform the old routine, the previous habit. By "unknowingly," it means without conscious thought; an example is breathing: we know we are breathing, but we do not have to consciously think about inhaling each breath of oxygen and exhaling each breath of carbon dioxide; we just do it without conscious thought.

The unconscious thought, or subconscious thought, or non-conscious thought, as it is also known, is what will form reality. It was this non-conscious habit that greatly helped form our current path.

Earl Nightingale said it well with this quote: "Whatever we plant in our subconscious mind and nourish with repetition and emotion will one day become a reality."[11]

This is not said to worry or scare anyone, because we are not stuck with the habits we have today. No, far from it. We can change them, we can change our world, and we can change the path our current destiny is on. We have the choice to break bad habits and create new and better ones for our lives.

If we want to change a bad habit, or any habit, we must not allow our thoughts to accept a lie as truth; we will also call lies myths because myths are, according to Merriam-Webster, "a popular belief" built upon "an unfounded or false notion."[12] I think this fits well with what we are talking about. Also, I like the sound of the word "myth" for this purpose better than "lies."

A myth about habits (about behavior) and about why we might do the same thing over and over in the same situation is the overused saying, "That's just how they are." We might also hear a similar version: "That's just who they are." I do not believe these sayings are completely true. A habit is a learned behavior; habits are not necessarily "how" a person is or "who" a person is. "How" is just an indicator of the manner or extent to which a person would say or do something. "Who" is a reference to a person's identity, which is a way we label people based on our perception of their reputation. A habit is just a result of numerous decisions, usually little and viewed as inconsequential, over a certain period of time.

"We choose the habits we form."

Habit is not something we change when we are motivated, because motivation is temporary and reliant upon a feeling which is also temporary and reliant upon our decision from an outside force. So, if we wait until we feel motivated to break, change, or create a new habit, then we will never fully break, change, or create a new habit. No. Habit is something that is consistent; first consciously planted and then unconsciously forming.

So, it is not "just who you are." You are more

than your current habits. You are more than your current behavior. You are not dictated by your habit; your habit is dictated by you.

Behavioral scientist and author BJ Fogg said it well when he said, "If you plant the right seed in the right spot, it will grow without further coaxing...The "right seed" is the tiny behavior that you choose. The "right spot" is the sequencing – what it comes after. The "coaxing" part is amping up motivation, which I think has nothing to do with creating habits. In fact, focusing on motivation as the key to habits is exactly wrong...If you pick the right small behavior and sequence it right, then you won't have to motivate yourself to have it grow. It will just happen naturally, like a good seed planted in a good spot."[13]

Habits are essential to our lives. They free up our cognitive mind for growth, adventure, entertainment, education, and human innovation by allowing the unconscious to drive most of our daily actions. Without habits, we would be forced to consciously think about and remind ourselves of even the most basic of survival needs, such as breathing, chewing, walking, and blinking. We would not have the time, function, or possibly even the energy to grow or advance ourselves or the human race. Good habits are vital to life and essential to reaching our good destiny. It is the bad habits that can be self-defeating and, much like an anchor to our lives, hold us back from forward progress toward our goals, our dreams, and our positive destiny. It is these habits that we tend to give no attention to until our conscious, yet inattentive, thoughts have created them and our repetitive actions have moved us into this behavioral pattern of the habit.

They tend to sneak up on us with no cause for attention until they are so ingrained that the appearance is that our habits own us. Or, as Samuel Johnson put it, "The chains of habit are too weak to be felt until they are too strong to be broken."[14] Really, I think it should read "until they appear, or feel, too heavy or too strong to be broken" because, as I have already mentioned, it is not easy, but they can be broken.

I repeat an act so it becomes a fact
That I will become the one I wish to be.
I must change my mind to view this life,
Not the one I was, but the future fact,
That through this tough and struggle strife
I will change my path, my character shall be
In line with the destiny that I know is fact.
I think, I speak, I act, I repeat, and I shall be.[15]

So, what habits do you have that might need to be changed?

What is it you want to accomplish?

What do you want to change in your life?

What type of person do you want to be?

Think about that, then begin to create those habits and replace those bad habits so that the new and good habits will lead you to those goals.

Remember, our brain—the unconscious mind—does not know the difference between a good and bad habit; it just does. That is why it is up to each of us to choose for ourselves if we will have the proper attitude, be committed to the time and effort it will take to change a habit, and if we will have the patience to allow this process to form.

Effort. Commitment. Patience.

I hope we can all listen to the words of this retired statesman and retired four-star general, Colin Powell, when he says, "If you are going to achieve excellence in big things, you develop the habit in little matters. Excellence is not an exception, it is a prevailing attitude."[16]

"A man's character is his fate."[1]

Heraclitus

CHAPTER 6

CHARACTER

The roads were eerily empty as Sam drove his brand-new Mercedes-Benz convertible along the oceanside highway. This road was usually traversed by many people out for a cruise on one of the numerous beautiful California days, but today it seemed as if Sam was the only person left on earth. He appeared to have the entire world to himself. He was not bothered by this; on the contrary, this is what he was hoping for when he made his plan for his five o'clock in the morning excursion to break in his new convertible toy. He was relishing this lazy-day drive, feeling the cool, salty wind blow through his hair and the warm morning sun shine on his face.

Sam just bought this vehicle with the money he earned from his modeling job. Sam is a model in two ways: his day job is the typical image one thinks of when they hear the term "male model"—he uses his masculine features and his well-trimmed, muscular figure to pose for photos while displaying new clothing lines for one of the most prominent clothing designers in the state; he is also a hand model— he uses his hands to help companies advertise their products. Sam makes very good money at these jobs, but this career choice does require a sacrifice in return; he must spend hours working out, eat healthy, and he must be very careful not to injure or damage his hands or face. These sacrifices are time-consuming and sometimes irritable sacrifices for Sam, but they are sacrifices he is happy to make to continue to earn the money required to afford the lifestyle of luxury he currently enjoys.

After a few miles of peace and tranquility,

Sam glanced in his rear-view mirror and caught a glimpse of a vehicle approaching fast as it swerved all over the highway. This vehicle must have been going at least thirty miles over the speed limit. Within seconds the vehicle flew past him at such a rate of speed it appeared as a blur, with the exception of laughter heard and beer cans Sam noticed being thrown out the window. This vehicle zipped around the corner and then was gone.

"Crazy drunk drivers. They're going to get someone killed," Sam said to himself.

Not too long after, Sam noticed a second vehicle quickly gaining on him. This one was a well-worn and slightly smoking minivan.

Wow! These people must be in a hurry, thought Sam.

In the minivan was a middle-aged woman applying makeup and chugging coffee while attempting to steer her two-ton machine. The woman was Amy, a single mother of three who was running late for her third part-time job; one more strike against her, and she was told she would lose her job. She was already struggling to pay her rent, bills, and take care of her kids on her meager income. If she lost this job, she knew it would be very likely she could fall behind on her rent, and as her landlord had already bent over backwards to help her (he had recently informed her that he could not bend anymore), one more time being late, and she would be evicted. She would not allow her kids to go without or to be living on the streets if she could help it.

Amy eventually caught up to Sam, and, as Sam inquisitively watched her, she began to pass him on the shoulder of the highway as they reached another slight curve. Then Sam saw Amy slam on her brakes. This startled Sam so much that he instinctively slammed his brakes without even looking to see why. When they were both stopped, they saw skid marks on the road and a vehicle dangling from a bent and broken rail guard on the edge of the highway, half hanging over the edge and facing a hundred-foot drop. Immediately Sam realized this vehicle was the one that had passed him earlier, driven by the drunks that were speeding and swerving. Amy and Sam saw a spark ignite into a small flame on the vehicle as it dangled precariously over what could soon become the most scorching and darkest valley that the two occupants would ever experience on this earth.

They looked at the vehicle in shock and dismay, then at each other with a look of questioning on their faces, and then back to the wreck. As they sat, staring in amazement and shock, they began to hear screams for help coming from inside the vehicle.

Sam muttered to himself, "This cannot be happening. Is this real? I should help, but what if I fall, get cut, or worse, what if I get burned? My career could be over."

He looked over to Amy, who was monologuing to herself as well.

She was saying, "What should I do? My kids are depending on me. But I can't leave these people to die, can I? No. But this was their own fault for not being careful and responsible. I can't help it if someone else fell into a pit of their own doing. They did this themselves; they were careless. I'm sorry. I have to go. I can't be late."

And with that, Amy drove by the wreck and continued toward her destination.

As Sam watched Amy drive off, he said to himself, "It's the right thing to do."

Sam got out of his vehicle and ran to the sounds of those in need. As he reached the vehicle, the flame grew and burst into a blaze. There was now no way he would be able to help without at least getting burned himself. Sam leapt onto the back of the vehicle, hoping to add some counterweight to help balance the vehicle. He busted the back window and reached through the flames and into the vehicle to pull out the occupants.

"What do you want to change in your life? What type of person do you want to be?"

Our character is the sum total of our choices. It is who we have allowed ourselves to become. As the story we just read illustrates, when the world around us is collapsing, when our stresses and concerns are at capacity, and when we find ourselves under pressure, those are the times when our true character will reveal itself. Will we be able to show love and self-control by keeping our emotions and our personal desires in check and not just think about or talk about the concerns and well-being of another but actually act upon those concerns? It is important to note that to be a person of good character does not mean we always put ourselves, our loved ones, or those for whom we are responsible at risk, day in and day out, nor does it mean we never make a mistake. Mistakes happen, errors in our judgment occur, and, sometimes, our awareness is lacking—sometimes, because we are humans, in some seasons and situations, we are just plain ignorant. Rather, to be a person of good character means we have built and understand our foundation, we work at and strive to make the right ethical and moral choices, and when we fail at this, we discern our faults and work toward correcting them and getting back on the right path toward the person we want to become.

In the story we read, Amy's priorities were first and foremost herself and her children. This is not typically a bad thing, but she assigned more worth to herself and her children's quality of life than she did to life itself. Sam, on the other hand, assigned more worth to the lives of those trapped in the vehicle than to the quality of life he was currently living.

What is it you are creating with your thoughts?

What are you inspiring in this world through your words?

What path are you choosing to move along based on your actions?

What type of person are you allowing to form from your habits?

Who is it you want your character to be?

According to the Bible, Adam and Eve were the first people to embark on this journey of character and destiny. They were created in paradise and had only one command to follow: "…you must not eat from the tree of the knowledge of good and evil…"[2] God loved them and wanted their destiny to be peace, joy, and a life without struggle, but He knew that love could not truly exist without freedom and liberty and that they could not and would not understand or fully appreciate these things if they were not free to choose. Thus, we have free will.

As the story goes, the serpent used its

words to fill Eve's thoughts with doubt and negativity about God's command, His love, and the creation of the fruit of this tree. Through thoughts of selfish pride, the serpent was able to fill Eve's head with egotistical views of grandeur—to fully know, understand, and be like God himself. As Obadiah 1:3 says, "The pride of your heart has deceived you."[3] Eve lost her humility and gave in to selfish pride. Eve then used her words to influence Adam, and they both took action in defiance of God's command.

In our thoughts, we create; in our words, we inspire; and in our actions, we move.

Though they had a momentary lapse of judgment in their character, they chose not to stop there. Now their souls knew good and evil, but their minds did not understand and could not yet process this new concept. Their lack of knowledge helped cause their character to rapidly decline, and without character, one can easily be swayed by doubt, confusion, wickedness, and fear. Well, they continued with their defiant actions, and through their words and thoughts, they created the habit of lying and accusation.

When Adam was confronted by God for his actions, God was giving Adam an opportunity to honestly account for his recent actions. He was giving Adam a second chance, an opportunity to acknowledge his fault and begin the path to correcting his error—to learn from his mistake, to change his thought process back to what is good and positive, and "whatever is noble, whatever is right, whatever is pure, whatever is lovely, whatever is admirable."[4] In this moment, when the world as he knew it was collapsing and he was under a new and unexplainable feeling of pressure from doubt, confusion, and fear that were squeezing his soul, Adam revealed who he had allowed himself to become; he revealed his character and changed the path toward his destiny, from life to death, and the rest, as they say, is history.

Character, just like thought, habits, and destiny, can be shaped and corrected, and who we have allowed ourselves to become can be renewed. The thoughts we think create, the words we speak inspire, the actions we take move, and the habits we conduct form who we will be, and together they build our character. Through positive and uplifting thoughts, we can begin to create the character we may desire in ourselves. "…be transformed by the renewing of your mind…"[5] However, we must put in the effort, have the commitment, and have patience, because just wishing or intending to be of good character will not work.

"Our character is the sum total of our choices."

There is a tragic story about a passenger jet that was shot down over the Kamchatka Peninsula, killing two hundred and sixty-nine people because of mechanical and human error and a choice of character. In 1983, commercial Korean Air Lines Flight KE007, also known as KAL Flight 007, was traveling from New York to Seoul, South Korea, but flew off course and accidently ended up in the airspace of the Soviet Union. This was during the Cold War, so tensions were already high, and unnamed aircraft in Soviet airspace were an almost certain disaster waiting to happen.

The Soviet pilot patrolling the airspace that night was Lieutenant Colonel Gennadi Osipovich. As the research into this incident goes, Lt. Col. Osipovich was not scheduled for duty that fateful night; he volunteered for that shift so he would have his schedule open during the day for a speech he was to give at his daughter's school. During his shift, he came into contact with the Korean Air Lines flight inside Soviet airspace. He stated that he was close enough to the aircraft to notice windows, lights, and the design of the aircraft. He stated that based on what he saw, he knew this aircraft was a 747-commercial airliner; however, based on the statement that no reply transmission was received from the aircraft, he said he suspected it could have been a trick to spy on their nuclear base. Either way, he was ordered to shoot it down. He followed those orders, and two hundred and sixty-nine people on a commercial flight that accidentally flew into the wrong airspace lost their lives. This act of military combativeness not only cost the lives of those on the flight but came close to causing a major disaster among world leaders, particularly the United States and Russia. What is worse is that the speech Lt. Col. Osipovich was scheduled to give was supposedly about peace; he was going to talk to the children and hopefully teach them about peace.[6, 7]

The words of his speech and his reasons for choosing to speak about peace are unknown to me, but what can be deduced from this story is that a person's character is more than just the words he speaks or the actions he takes. I am sure Lt. Col. Osipovich had good, and possibly the best, intentions in preparing to teach the children about peace, but good intentions are not enough to make a lasting impact or bring one about and fulfill their positive destiny. Character, true character, cannot be measured or supported by words or actions alone, and neither can it be supported by good intentions. Good intentions can be delivered through ill-gotten means; good intentions can be similar to the old saying, "The ends justify the means." Good intentions are not always the right thing to do. Good intentions do not define character.

Well, then, what is character?

According to Merriam-Webster, "character" is "one of the attributes or features that make up and distinguish an individual," "a feature used to separate distinguishable things into categories," and "mental and ethical traits marking and often individualizing a person."[8]

However, I think Dr. Mark Rutland, a busy man with the titles of missionary, evangelist, ordained minister, and president of Global

Servants, said it best in his book *Character Matters* when he said, "Character, the composite of virtues and values…"[9]

I agree with this, but I think there is another aspect that must be added to virtue and values to find true character.

Character, to me, is a blend of the values one chooses to live their life by, the virtues by which one conducts their life, and the integrity by which one holds themselves to. True character is an alignment of value, virtue, and integrity.

When I say "true character," I am referring to a good character in the sense of love, care, generosity, compassion, servanthood, etc.; someone most of us would consider a good person.

However, a person could have integrity in their virtues that lines up perfectly with their values and still be a bad or evil person if their values are foul.

"Through positive and uplifting thoughts, we can begin to create the character we may desire in ourselves."

"What?" I know, you're probably asking, "Could you maybe be like the chicken that stopped in the middle of the road and lay it on the line?" I thought the same thing when this realization came to me, so let me elaborate on this just a bit.

By "value," I mean the quality given to our lives by what we choose to live by; it is what we choose as our moral compass. Morality is the doctrine by which we conform our lives, our ideals, our beliefs, and our ideas of what is actually right or wrong. Morals are what our verity is built upon. Value comes from our foundation. So, the question here, in terms of value, is: what is your foundation? What is the cornerstone on which you build your life?

By "virtue," I mean the way in which we behave when it comes to our view of what is right and what is wrong. It is our habit that forms our behavior; this habit is created by our thoughts of who we are, inspired by the words we speak over ourselves and our life, moved by our repeated actions, and formed by our daily habits to establish the standard—character—by which we live our life. As Dr. Mark Rutland eloquently put it, "virtue is restrained strength."[10] So, the question here is, will you have the discipline, strength, and courage to stand by your values and be virtuous?

By "integrity," I mean the capacity or degree to which our virtue adheres to and lines up with our value system. We are humans, and, as such, we are flawed, and in being flawed, we will stumble and have moments where we might slip in our integrity and not be as virtuous as we strive to be. It is in those tests, in those moments where our decision is paramount to keeping our core value, that the level of our integrity will truly be revealed. As mentioned previously, we will make mistakes, and there will be times when our integrity will be questioned, but it is not about never faltering but rather acknowledging the fault and working to correct it and better ourselves. Grace, forgiveness, help, correction, and willful intent are important for each of us in those moments of frailty. So, the question here is, will you strive to be a person of strong integrity?

A person can have a good, or righteous, value system and live with virtue but still have little integrity if the degree to which their habit, the true habit that is not consciously and temporarily restrained for the public, lines up with their values is disproportionate and thus lacks true character.

A person can have a good, or righteous, value system and have strong integrity yet still lack the virtue, or habit, by which they behave based on their values and thus lacks true character.

A person can have great integrity and live a life of virtue but have a warped, or bad, or wicked (you choose the word), or shaky value system and thus lacks true character.

> *"It is in those tests, in those moments where our decision is paramount to keeping our core value, that the level of our integrity will truly be revealed."*

Our character is the heart of who we truly have become. It is what was built upon the foundation of our current values and is the accumulation of our thoughts, words, actions, and habits.

So, what behavior have your habits created for you that is helping to form your character?

One must be willing to get deep and honest with oneself in order to find this answer.

When you do, is your character good?

Is your character built on a strong foundation?

Is it true?

Is it who you want to be?

Many years ago, I was honored to be a part of an independent feature film. This was a nerve-wracking and stressful experience, mostly because I truly saw the two leads as Hollywood-level actors, and I was still learning.

The character I was to portray was a minor character, meaning he had a name and lines and contributed to the progression of the plot in the story; however, because of the work I put into figuring out his life, it turned into a bigger role. I created a backstory for my character so I could, hopefully, better understand his actions and reasons for being in the story. For every scene he was in, I marked up those pages on my script with what he was thinking, how long he was thinking it, and why. Then I looked at his words written in the script and decided whether or not they aligned with the thought and why. Then, I marked what I thought his actions would be based on his thinking. Then, when I saw that most of his words did not line up with what I thought would be going on in his mind, I created some habits for him, such as not making eye contact and changing his posture.

His thoughts created the person he would become—a good or bad character. His words either inspired or discouraged him. His actions moved him to the people and places that would help him continue on the path his thoughts were creating. His character was formed and shaped, and it was this portrayal that showed his character not just being formed but revealing itself throughout the story. This is what I think helped bring this character from the background to the foreground. I truly think it was not my delivery of lines (this was prior to what I mentioned in Chapter 2, so I was still trying to figure that part out) but the character, or portrayal of his true character, that made him come to life and grab the heart of the original writer.

Honestly, the importance of character and the gradual reveal of this character's character through his thoughts, words, and actions was something I would not figure out or understand for years. I was doing all that work and studying for the character because I was hoping to impress the two leads and because I was confused. I did not understand the role at first, and that confusion led me to all that research. As I stated in the previous chapter, it is the confusion that typically leads me to do a lot of research and, usually, grows my understanding.

It took a lot of work to build my character in that film, just as it takes work to build our character in real life. As Heraclitus is quoted, "Good character is not formed in a week or a month. It is created little by little, day by day. Protracted and patient effort is needed to develop good character."[11] It's like sanctification;

it's a process, and one of its meanings is "to set apart" or "being purified"[12]—purified from our nearly eighty percent negative thinking to a more positive destiny. However, just as in every story, we see that evil never gives up without a fight, and neither will negativity give up so easily, but it can be defeated. The character, as with any character in any story, faced suffering in his story, and with that he dealt with the same decisions we do: the choice to think, speak, act, and behave as he would choose to allow himself to, and in doing so, he began to change his thinking, which changed his speech, which changed his actions, and, in the end, changed his destiny. As it says, "we [rejoice] in our sufferings, because we know that suffering produces perseverance; perseverance, character; and character [good character], hope."[13]

The VIA, or "Values in Action, Classification of Character Strengths and Virtues," is the classification of six main categories, or what they called "virtues," and 24-character traits that were determined in 2004 by a group of scientists who were studying the science of character. What interested me in this study was their determination that what they called "virtues" and "character traits" were what determined a person's character. They also determined that a person's character could be developed and shaped regardless of their circumstances. Supposedly, according to their research and findings, we begin to shape and build our character in our prefrontal cortex, which is the part of the brain where we control our cognition, personality, critical thinking (or decision-making), and self-control.[14, 15] By changing our thoughts, by controlling our mouth and the words we allow to exit, by exercising self-control in our actions, and by forming good habits, we can effectively shape our character and be the person we desire; we can become a person of good and true character.

We can change our path and who we are. It does not matter how much time we have let slip away or how far we have let our character fall;

we are in charge of who we become, and we must choose who that is.

We must get open and honest with ourselves and pay attention to our true character, for our reputation is what others might confuse as our character, and one's reputation might not always be interpreted correctly. Our reputation is the perceived portrayal of us that is noticed during the brief instances others might witness in our life; it is not the whole, hidden, or true character.

"Our character is the heart of who we truly have become."

If you are a little confused by this, it is okay, because others have said similar things in the past and said them much clearer than my mind organized it here. Here are two people who, I hope, can clear this up a bit more. Let us start with John Wooden: "Be more concerned with your character than your reputation, because your character is what you really are, while your reputation is merely what others think you are."[16] Abraham Lincoln put it another way: "Character is like a tree and reputation like a shadow. The shadow is what we think of it; the tree is the real thing."[17]

Who are you that walks before me?

What is it that you want?

Cautiously moving, what does thou foresee?

Why ignore me? You act nonchalant.

If you are here to guide my path

Then please, I beg, speak.

My thoughts, they all fall flat

And this path we walk is bleak.

I think we should take another route,

The one you walk, it is not straight;

I do not intend to anger or dispute,

But your reply I do await.

Please calm my fears and say something,

Just one word to follow through,

For this path is rough and what I think

Needs inspiration spoken to.

The dips and hills and rocky ground,

My feet, it makes, slip and twist.

With each step I take, the action pounds,

The more I move the less you exist.

I trust you know to what you lead me

As I repeat these steps and words.

Cautiously moving, what does thou foresee?

As we reach the end it confers.

It was not what you want from me,

But what I want for you.

And through this journey, I was always free

To think, speak, step, and change my view.[18]

So, are you the person people think you are?

Are you exercising your mind to think on thoughts of good, uplifting, optimistic, and positive things? How about gratitude?

Are you speaking words of influence into your life or words of discouragement?

Are your actions serving you and taking you in the direction you want?

Are your habits keeping you in a vicious cycle, or are they guiding you through the seasons of life while building upon your foundation and making you stronger?

Is your character who you want it to be and not just a fleeting image of what others imagine of you?

To be of good character takes effort, work, commitment, and time. Character is who you are; it is authentically you. Two-time NFL MVP, Aaron Rodgers, says it well: "Authenticity is everything! You have to wake up every day and look in the mirror, and you want to be proud of the person who's looking back at you. And you can only do that if you're being honest with yourself and being a person of high character. You have an opportunity every single day to write that story of your life."[19]

"It is not in the stars to hold our destiny but in ourselves."[1]

William Shakespeare

CHAPTER 7

DESTINY

Four aging gentlemen kneeled before their King in front of everyone, each wondering exactly why their presence was summoned. Three of them were imagining what wonderful gift their King might bestow upon them. Each, however, believed and was hoping they had no reason to worry because, in their own minds and lives, they reasoned, they were good servants who stewarded what they were given well and who did well in life, and by doing well they must be admired by their King for such success, ingenuity, and character. Besides, they reasoned with themselves, they've done more good deeds than bad ones, so their

King would notice, take that into account, and be very pleased. Each found an opportunity in every situation to grow themselves and their dreams while helping, as they justified it, their fellow countrymen.

One was a blacksmith who spent his days forging steel for shields, armor, and weapons for the knights of the kingdom; when he found out all these items were paid for not by the knights themselves but out of the Kings' treasure, he knowingly and willingly began cutting back on the manganese and other materials needed for the steel to fully harden and have strength. He also increased his prices until he only needed three months' service to live comfortably the rest of the year.

"Why not?" he told himself. "The knight's talent and skill in combat are what's most important, anyway. Not what I do. Also, the King can afford such absorbent prices, and the time and resources I have saved will help me and my family. It's my money; I need the money."

Another was a builder who built many of the dwelling places around the kingdom; he understood the cost of building and the importance of location, such as firm and solid ground. He had learned his trade from the master builder, and his excellence in this trade had caught the attention of the King, whom he was privileged to get to know. He had the third-best land behind the King and the farmer. In fact, he was able to obtain this land when the previous owners' reputation was severely damaged: it was said that the previous owner cheated his fellow countrymen out of proper materials, which was rumored to be the cause of continuous repairs. This builder, the man who now owned this land, knew most people knew nothing of building; thus, he was able to cut corners and build other people's homes on ground that was soft and unstable, allowing himself to obtain the next best piece of land and to profit from future repairs.

"Why not?" he told himself. "My competition is gone; I need the business, and they need a roof over their heads. It's job security. Besides, it's a win-win for all that matter."

"Our reputation is the perceived portrayal of us that is noticed during the brief instances others might witness in our life; it is not the whole, hidden, or true character."

The third was a peasant who made little working in the fields but never wanted for anything. However, he believed he was owed more for his work, and since he was not given what he felt he deserved, he slowed his work and burdened others with the load; he also felt entitled to take home some of the farmer's crop and other goods that were in others' possession. He reasoned that what the farmer had was given by the King, and since the King was the wealthiest in the land, if the farmer noticed something missing, he could just ask for another—no harm, no foul. He even stole food, goods, and medicine from his fellow peasants. In one instance, the medicine he stole cost the life of his neighbor.

"Why not?" he told himself. "I work hard so others can live in wealth and comfort. Besides, they can afford the loss; I can't. So, I'm only taking what I'm entitled to; I'm owed this stuff; I want what I deserve; and "charity" is good for them."

The fourth was the farmer, who hired the peasant and ran the farmland for the kingdom. He was blessed with what he had in life and chose to use that blessing to help others. He employed others in the kingdom to work the crops and fields for an agreeable wage. His workers never went without, and he even generously helped others throughout the kingdom.

As these men waited for their King to speak, they grew more and more anxious for what they assumed might be coming to them.

As the King rose, he looked out among the people and shouted, "I called you before me today to make a point to all the people of this land. There will be those who may acquire more in this life, such as I and three of the men before me, just as there will be those who may toil for scraps as one of these men lives."

With that statement, the peasant smiled big as he thought to himself, *Surely he is acknowledging my meager lifestyle. These other men are of wealth and status, so he must be talking about me. Finally, justice is coming. I am going to receive my reward for all my hard work. I deserve this reward, whatever it may be. It is rightfully mine.*

The King continued, "The blacksmith here before me has earned great wealth forging weapons and armor for our knights in battle."

The blacksmith smirked at the other three men and smiled big.

The King pointed his scepter toward the blacksmith and said, "He has also drained a portion of the kingdom's wealth for his own greed. Not only that, but he has, under oath to his King, lied about the quality of the goods he was paid to create. In doing so, our knights have less armor and even fewer weapons to defend this kingdom with than ever before, and the quality of these items has become weak and broken, and our guardians no longer wear full protective armor; because of this, many needlessly fell in defense of our kingdom. His is a character of false testimony and self-serving greed."

The blacksmith's smile quickly vanished, and he began to sweat.

The King looked toward his loyal guards and said, "Take everything he has and give it to the families of our knights who fell in battle."

The blacksmith begged, "But your Majesty…"

"Depart from me," interrupted the King.

The blacksmith was escorted out of the kingdom.

The King then looked toward the builder and said, "The builder here before me has helped many people in this kingdom."

The builder smiled big with this accolade.

"However," the King continued, "he has stolen the best land for himself and has willfully and knowingly built shoddy dwellings on unsuitable land for the purpose of sustaining his own business and lifestyle. He even falsely ruined the life of someone who served us well. Because of this, many of our fellow countrymen live in further poverty, and others have perished in the storms. His is a character of pride, slander, selfishness, and fear," said the King.

The builder's face turned white, and he too began to sweat.

"Take everything he has and give it to those who have lost everything in the storms," declared the King.

"But it's me, your Majesty," the builder whimpered. "Have I not built monuments in your name?"

The King answered, "I never knew you."

The builder was escorted out of the kingdom.

The King continued his speech, "The peasant here before me works every day toiling in the fields, harvesting the crops that fill the bellies of all in this kingdom."

The peasant smiled big and even risked turning around to see the looks of all those in the crowd, for he was relishing in this seemingly pleasant and boastful praise.

Then the King said, "Although he lacked no essentials required to live and was given more than he needed, he still coveted what others had. His wants and lusts for what he felt was due him led him to a subversive nature toward his work, his employer, his fellow man, and his King, and with this he chose thievery and deceit. He pined, and his appetency for more drove him to watch as he acted with selfishness to fuel his false thinking as another died when he needlessly took what this person needed to live. His is a character of thievery, murder, and unprincipled, unworthy, self-centered, entitlement mentality."

The peasant shrank in his posture, lowering his eyes, and he too began to sweat.

The King looked to his loyal guards and said, "Take everything this man has and give it to the family of the one he let die. Also, take this man out of my sight and out of the kingdom."

> *"Are your actions serving you and taking you in the direction you want?"*

Then the King looked to the farmer and

said, "This man before you is a farmer. He was granted much land, wealth, and favor in this kingdom. Using his talents with his gift, he has produced much food and helped bless countless people."

The farmer lowered his head at this proclamation, knowing that all that he had been granted and was in his possession was now gone. He no longer owned the land, the crops, or had any wealth; in fact, he was now poorer than the lowest peasant. He was broke and without a home of his own. He knew the king would not be happy with this. The King granted him and him alone this honor and wealth, and he had invested it all in what now appeared to look as if he had just traded it all.

The King continued, "This man before you has lost all that was granted to him."

Now, the farmer began to sweat. He was sure the King would order his execution any time now.

"He knew someone was deceiving the

records," said the King, "and he knew thievery was happening on his watch. He even came to me and told me who he believed was doing this and why he believed they were."

The farmer began to tremble.

The King looked among the people and said, "However, he had compassion for his fellow man, and he showed love and goodwill toward this man, extending mercy and grace by continuously paying his debt from his own earnings. He even paid above and beyond so that the extra food and goods you all enjoy would be possible."

"He saw the orphans scattered as their dwelling place collapsed, and he paid for the builder to repair their orphanage," stated the King. He continued, "He heard the cries from the widows of our brave knights who fell in battle and did what he could to alleviate their burdens. He felt the hunger pains of his fellow countrymen who were starving because the food supply was disappearing and he gave the food from his own table to fill your bellies."

The King extended his sceptor toward the farmer and said, "This man now lives in squalor; he has burdened himself with the most debt and now owns nothing, not even his own life. He gave it all away so that his fellow countrymen might live happier, healthier, and freer lives, and not once did he complain or demand anything from any of you in return except for honest work. His is truly a character of love, goodness, faithfulness, gentleness, self-control, and kindness."

The King looked at the farmer, smiled, and declared, "And for this, for having true character, I will now reward him with everlasting joy; all his debts are now forgiven, and he shall live like my son, and he shall never want again."

Your destiny is determined by you.

Who do you want to be?

What character do you want for yourself?

What do you want for your life?

Think about it, and let it be created in your thoughts. Make it clear. Speak it into life with words of positivity and inspiration. Move toward that creation with your actions. Form good habits that will help you reach that goal and form your true character—a good character. Then, let your character shape the destiny you desire.

Our destiny is determined by the choices we make.

In our thoughts, we create our destiny; with our words, we inspire our destiny; through our actions, we move toward our destiny; because of our repeated habits, we form our destiny; and based on the character we have allowed ourselves to become, we shape and live our destiny.

Rich or Poor, Life or Death, you get to choose your destiny.

ABOUT THE AUTHOR

Josh likes to laugh, which means he has emotions. Emotions mean he is human; and being human, he has experienced the ups and downs, the joys and pains, of this life just like everyone else. Through it all, he has chosen to write about what he has learned with the hope of helping others reach higher levels, find their success, and see hope by changing their perspective for a better understanding.

Josh C. Jones has a Bachelor's of Science in Media, graduating Cum Laude from Oral Roberts University.

Josh has been nominated and won some awards for his work in photography, filmmaking, and acting, and he has had one of his poems published while he was just a small child—though it was published under his brother's name (a story for another time).

Josh has garnered much life experience working in various fields—housekeeping, education, retail, sports and live video production, film and entertainment, theater, campus police, entrepreneur, business owner, podcaster, speaker, and more—which has helped him learn and build the knowledge, understanding, character, and wisdom he has today that he wishes to share with you through his writings.

As Josh has learned—sometimes the hard way—and likes to repeat in his writings: we learn more through our perceived failures than victories, and because of our willingness to engage with others, our perspective enlarges. It is through his perceived failures and because he has been blessed to meet and work with many well-known and successful people from whom he has gained further insights and learned to see things from new perspectives, that he hopes to help others be better, reach higher, find their footing on a firm foundation, reach their success, and find hope.

The first edition of this book, which was titled *Destiny: Life or Death, Choose Your Destiny*, was Josh's first book to be published, and as an added bonus, it was published by an actual publishing company—a blessing that only a few achieve, especially for being a first-time author, and a blessing for which he is forever grateful.

Josh C. Jones is an author (a title he can now happily and graciously state) with more books already written and in the queue just waiting their turn to be read by you; and a few, since the first publication of this book, already published and ready to be placed in your hands.

ENTREPRENEUR: Road Map For Success, Five Characteristics of the Successful and Respected, his second book to be published, was signed and published by a second publishing company—another blessing he never saw coming but one he is, once again, extremely grateful and thankful for. God is good! What is this book about? This book breaks down the five characteristics that can greatly help lead you to success and respect in this world. You can actively choose to incorporate and build these characteristics into your daily life—characteristics that will produce positive results and help you build your self-worth, achieve your dream, reach your success, and live a life worthy of respect. Now is the time for you to be the entrepreneur of your life. Now is the time for you to achieve your success.

Making sense of America's newest Guild... Again: What I discovered in my search for answers. What is this book about? We've wondered, haven't we?

What is it, really? That's why I decided to ask questions and seek to discover answers. In this book, you will read about what I have learned and discovered through my conversations with people when it comes to the question I believe we've all asked: What is MAGA? Is it truly that complex or strange, or might there actually be a common thread by which we can begin to stitch our home back together?

AMERICA Then and Now: a poem by Josh C. Jones. What is this book about? This is a longer poem that reflects on what America was founded to be, what we once knew was truth, and what we've allowed it to evolve into. This poem is a reflection of the seeds of the past that were planted and watered by our Founders and how, over time, infiltration of germination from some of the very weeds our Founders warned have sprouted "fundamental change" to originality, revising text, pluralizing truth, strangling freedom's roots, and distorting the reality of moral principles. In the end, you get to decide which "truth" you will salute.

Josh has a passion to help bring the truth, better understanding, hope, and entertainment to people through his writing and creativity. You can hear Josh C. Jones offer further insights and perspectives for free on his podcast *From My Standpoint*, which can be found on Apple Podcasts, Spotify, and most podcast listening platforms, where he hopes to change the perspective for a better understanding.

You can also visit Josh C. Jones' website at www.JoshCJonesAuthor.com to contact him and view all of his published work, blogs, and podcast episodes.

BIBLIOGRAPHY

CHAPTER 1

PROLOGUE

1. "Tony Robbins Quotes." BrainyQuote. com. BrainyMedia Inc, 2019. 29 June 2019. https://www.brainyquote.com/quotes/tony_robbins_147787

2. "H. Jackson Brown, Jr. Quotes." Brainy-Quote.com. BrainyMedia Inc, 2022. 31 December 2022. https://www.brainy-quote.com/quotes/h_jackson_brown_jr_382774

3. Quote by Dr. Dave Leggett, during a business meeting.

4. 1977 May 18, San Antonio Light, What They're Saying, Quote Page 7-B (NArch Page 28), Column 4, San Antonio, Texas. (NewspaperArchive)

CHAPTER 2

THOUGHTS

1. "Robert H. Schuller Quotes." Brainy-Quote.com. BrainyMedia Inc, 2019. 16 May 2019. https://www.brainyquote. com/quotes/robert_h_schuller_120987

2. "Marcus Aurelius Quotes." Brainy-Quote.com. BrainyMedia Inc, 2017. 7 May 2017. https://www.brainyquote. com/quotes/marcus_aurelius_148747

3. "Ralph Waldo Emerson Quotes." BrainyQuote.com. BrainyMedia Inc, 2017. 7 May 2017. https://www.brainy-quote.com/quotes/ralph_waldo_emer-son_108797

4. Napoleon Hill, *Think and Grow Rich.* Electronic Facsimile Edition. (Meriden, Connecticut: The Ralston Society, 1938, 2000).

5. Will Durant. *The Greatest Minds and Ideas of All Time.* (New York, NY: Simon & Schuster, 2002).

6. "thought." *Merriam-Webster.com.* Merri-

am-Webster, 2017. Web. 27 July 2017.

7. Kevin Daum, "35 Quotes on Endings That Will Make 2016 More," *Inc*.com, retrieved from the Internet on September 18, 2018 at https://www.inc.com/kevin-daum/35-quotes-on-ending-things-that-will-make-2016-more-exciting.html

8. Steve Maraboli. *Life, the Truth, & Being Free.* (Port Washington, NY: A Better Today, 2014).

9. Earl Nightingale. *The Strangest Secret.* (Shippensburg, PA: Sound Wisdom, 2019).

10. "Jean-Paul Sartre Quotes." BrainyQuote.com. BrainyMedia Inc, 2017. 27 July 2017. https://www.brainyquote.com/quotes/jeanpaul_sartre_382253

11. Betty J. Eadie. *Embraced by the Light.* Bantam Edition. (Placerville, CA: Gold Leaf Press, 1994).

12. Neringa Antanaityte, "Mind Matters: How To Effortlessly Have More Positive Thoughts," *TLEX* Institute, retrieved from the Internet on September 24, 2018 at https://tlexinstitute.com/how-to-effortlessly-have-more-positive-thoughts/

13. The Holy Bible, New International Version. Grand Rapids: Zondervan House, 1984. Print.

    a. Philippians 4:8

14. "What Is Neuroplasticity?," Brain Works, retrieved from the Internet on February 13, 2019 at https://brainworksneurotherapy.com/what-neuroplasticity

15. Katherine Harmon, "It's a Solid… It's a Liquid… It's Oobleck!," *Scientific American*, retrieved from the Internet on March 30, 2018 at https://www.scientificamerican.com/article/oobleck-bring-science-home/

16. "Werner Heisenberg," *The Physics of the Universe*, retrieved from the Internet on October 12, 2018 at https://www.physicsoftheuniverse.com/scientists_heisenberg.html

17. Feb 12, 2016 (Sparrow Quote, Russian Proverb) "Sparrow Sayings and Sparrow Quotes: Wise Old Sayings," *Wise Old Sayings*, retrieved from the Internet on July 22, 2019 at http://www.wiseoldsayings.com/sparrow-quotes/

18. "Rudyard Kipling Quotes." BrainyQuote.com. BrainyMedia Inc, 2016. 12 February 2016. https://www.brainyquote.com/quotes/rudyard_kipling_101386

19. Poem by Josh C. Jones

20. The Holy Bible, New International Version. Grand Rapids: Zondervan House, 1984. Print.

   a. Philippians 4:8

21. Bryn Farnsworth, "Human Behavior: The Complete Pocket Guide," *imotions*, retrieved from the Internet on July 10, 2019 at https://imotions.com/blog/human-behavior/

22. Quote by Dr. Dave Leggett, during a business meeting.

23. George Orwell. *1984*. (New York, NY: New American Library, 1961).

24. "Oliver Wendell Holmes, Sr. Quotes." BrainyQuote.com. BrainyMedia Inc, 2016. 12 February 2016. https://www.brainyquote.com/quotes/oliver_wendell_holmes_sr_122641

CHAPTER 3

WORDS

1. "Oliver Wendell Holmes, Sr. Quotes." BrainyQuote.com. BrainyMedia Inc, 2019. 29 June 2019. https://www.

brainyquote.com/quotes/oliver_wen-
dell_holmes_sr_122641

2. Adapted from a story found: Stephen, "Encouragement Story – A Group of Frogs," *Motivational Stories*, retrieved from the Internet on December 17, 2018 at https://academictips.org/blogs/encouragement-story-a-group-of-frogs/

3. "The Significant Problems We Face Cannot Be Solved at the Same Level of Thinking We Were at When We Created Them." *Albert Einstein: The Significant Problems We Face Cannot Be Solved at the Same Level of Thinking We Were at When We Created Them.*, https://www.quotes.net/quote/9226.

4. James C. Humes. *Speak like Churchill Stand like Lincoln: 21 Powerful Secrets of History's Greatest Speakers.* (New York: Prima Publishing, 2002).

5. Richard Lederer. *The Miracle of Language.*

New York, NY: Pocket Books, 1991).

6. "Nathaniel Hawthorne Quotes." BrainyQuote.com. BrainyMedia Inc, 2019. 9 May 2019. https://www.brainy-quote.com/quotes/nathaniel_haw-thorne_108644

7. The Holy Bible, New International Version. Grand Rapids: Zondervan House, 1984. Print.

   a. Proverbs 18:21

8. The Holy Bible, New International Version. Grand Rapids: Zondervan House, 1984. Print.

   a. Proverbs 18:21

9. The Holy Bible, New International Version. Grand Rapids: Zondervan House, 1984. Print.

   a. James 3:3-5

10. Robert Greene. *The 48 Laws of Power.* (New York, NY: Penguin Books, 2000).

11. The Holy Bible, New International Version. Grand Rapids: Zondervan House, 1984. Print.

    a. Proverbs 15:4

12. Shakko, wikipedia U. "**Aesop**." *Ancient History Encyclopedia.* Ancient History Encyclopedia, 08 Mar 2014. Web. 29 Jun 2019.

13. The Holy Bible, New International Version. Grand Rapids: Zondervan House, 1984. Print.

    a. Proverbs 18:6-7

14. "Word." *Merriam-Webster.com.* Merriam-Webster, 2017. Web. 8 May 2017.

15. The Holy Bible, New International Version. Grand Rapids: Zondervan House, 1984. Print.

    a. James 1:19

16. "Robert Southey Quotes." BrainyQuote.com. BrainyMedia Inc, 2016. 12 Feb-

ruary 2016. https://www.brainyquote.
com/quotes/robert_southey_155607

17. The Holy Bible, New International Version. Grand Rapids: Zondervan House, 1984. Print.

   a. James 3:5

18. "Dante Alighieri Quotes." BrainyQuote.com. BrainyMedia Inc, 2022. 22 December 2022. https://www.brainyquote.com/quotes/dante_alighieri_379813

19. "Albert Schweitzer Quotes." BrainyQuote.com. BrainyMedia Inc, 2022. 22 December 2022. https://www.brainyquote.com/quotes/albert_schweitzer_402282

20. "Charles R. Swindoll Quotes." BrainyQuote.com. BrainyMedia Inc, 2022. 24 December 2022. https://www.brainyquote.com/quotes/charles_r_swindoll_388332

21. The Holy Bible, New International Ver-

sion. Grand Rapids: Zondervan House, 1984. Print.

    a. Matthew 8:28, 31-32

22. James C. Humes. *Speak like Churchill Stand like Lincoln: 21 Powerful Secrets of History's Greatest Speakers.* (New York: Prima Publishing, 2002).

23. The Holy Bible, New International Version. Grand Rapids: Zondervan House, 1984. Print.

    a. Proverbs 17:28

24. The Holy Bible, New International Version. Grand Rapids: Zondervan House, 1984. Print.

    a. James 2:17

25. "Beliefnet's Inspirational Quotes," *Beliefnet*, retrieved from the Internet on May 20, 2018 at https://www.beliefnet.com/quotes/entertainment/s/sammy-hagar/words-have-power-they-work-thats-

why-poetry-can.aspx

26. Masaru Emoto. *The Hidden Messages in Water*. (Hillsboro, Oregon: Beyond Words Publishing, Inc., 2004).

27. Reiko Myamoto Dewey. "More Messages in Water with Dr. Masaru Emoto," *Spirit of Ma'at*, retrieved from the Internet on May 20, 2018 at http://www.spiritofmaat.com/archive/nov1/cwater.htm

28. The Holy Bible, New International Version. Grand Rapids: Zondervan House, 1984. Print.

   a. Joshua 1:8

29. Masaru Emoto. *The Hidden Messages in Water*. (Hillsboro, Oregon: Beyond Words Publishing, Inc., 2004).

30. The Holy Bible, New International Version. Grand Rapids: Zondervan House, 1984. Print.

a. Philippians 4:8

31. Poem by Josh C. Jones

32. Colin Cherry. On Human Communication: A Review, A Survey, and a Criticism. Third Edition. (Cambridge, Massachusetts: The Massachusetts Institute of Technology, 1978).

33. Irving J. Lee. The Language of Wisdom and Folly: Background Readings in Semantics. (New York: Harper & Brothers Publishers, 1949).

34. CHERYLZ1961, "Reckless Words," *Inspirational Christian Blogs*, retrieved from the Internet on July 12, 2016 at https://www.inspirationalchristianblogs.com/2014/11/02/reckless-words/

CHAPTER 4

ACTIONS

1. "Thich Nhat Hanh Quotes." Brainy-

Quote.com. BrainyMedia Inc, 2019. 16 May 2019. https://www.brainyquote. com/quotes/thich_nhat_hanh_531603

2. "Mark Twain Quotes." BrainyQuote. com. BrainyMedia Inc, 2018. 18 October 2018. https://www.brainyquote. com/quotes/mark_twain_162937

3. The Holy Bible, New International Version. Grand Rapids: Zondervan House, 1984. Print.

   a. James 2:17

4. "Obama interview March 22, 2008," *Mail* Tribune, retrieved from the internet on March 10, 2019 at https:// mailtribune.com/do-not-use-videos/ obama-interview-march-22-2008

5. Gavin Aronsen. "Feds Raid Oaksterdam University," *Mother* Jones, retrieved from the internet on March 10, 2019 https:// www.motherjones.com/crime-justice/2012/04/federal-raid-oakster-

dam-oakland-marijuana/

6. Washington Post Staff. "Full text: Donald Trump announces a presidential bid," *The Washington Post*, retrieved from the internet on March 10, 2019 at https://www.washingtonpost.com/news/post-politics/wp/2015/06/16/full-text-donald-trump-announces-a-presidential-bid/?noredirect=on&utm_term=.651e2f21676a

7. "Tara Brown." AZQuotes.com. Wind and Fly LTD, 2022. 31 December 2022. https://www.azquotes.com/quote/932546

8. "action." *Merriam-Webster.com*. Merriam-Webster, 2018. Web. 23 May 2018.

9. "Marcus Aurelius Quotes." BrainyQuote.com. BrainyMedia Inc, 2019. 10 July 2019. https://www.brainyquote.com/quotes/marcus_aurelius_148750

10. "Henri Bergson Quotes." BrainyQuote.

com. BrainyMedia Inc, 2022. 31 December 2022. https://www.brainyquote.com/quotes/henri_bergson_107149

11. The Holy Bible, New International Version. Grand Rapids: Zondervan House, 1984. Print.

    a. Matthew 5:47

12. Poem by Josh C. Jones

13. Rob Bell. *Sex God: Exploring the Endless Connections Between Sexuality and Spirituality*. (New York, NY: HarperCollins Publishers, 2012).

14. "Marcus Aurelius Quotes." BrainyQuote.com. BrainyMedia Inc, 2022. 31 December 2022. https://www.brainyquote.com/quotes/marcus_aurelius_131341

15. "Mark Twain Quotes." BrainyQuote.com. BrainyMedia Inc, 2018. 18 October 2018. https://www.brainyquote.com/quotes/mark_twain_162937

CHAPTER 5

HABITS

1. "Travis Bradberry Quotes." Brainy-Quote.com. BrainyMedia Inc, 2019. 16 May 2019. https://www.brainyquote. com/quotes/travis_bradberry_734882

2. Philosiblog. "You've Been Criticizing Yourself for Years and It Hasn't Worked. Try Approving of Yourself and See What Happens." *Philosiblog*, 2 Apr. 2014, https://philosiblog. com/2014/04/02/youve-been-criticizing-yourself-for-years-and-it-hasnt-worked-try-approving-of-yourself-and-see-what-happens/.

3. Phillippa Lally, Cornelia H. M. Van Jaarsveld, Henry W. W. Potts, Jane Wardle. "How are habits formed: Modelling habit formation in the real world." European Journal of Social Psychology.

(2009): 1002.

4. "habit." *Merriam-Webster.com*. Merriam-Webster, 2018. Web. 8 December 2018.

5. "behavior." *Merriam-Webster.com*. Merriam-Webster, 2018. Web. 8 December 2018.

6. "If Confusion Is the First Step to Knowledge, I Must Be a Genius." *Larry Leissner: If Confusion Is the First Step to Knowledge, I Must Be a Genius.*, www.quotes.net/quote/39775.

7. "Desmond Tutu Quotes." BrainyQuote.com. BrainyMedia Inc, 2023. 1 February 2023. https://www.brainyquote.com/quotes/desmond_tutu_454129

8. The Holy Bible, New International Version. Grand Rapids: Zondervan House, 1984. Print.

   a. Romans 8:24

9. Charles Duhigg. *The Power of Habit: Why We Do What We Do in Life and Business.* (New York: Random House, 2012).

10. "How Long Does It Really Take to Break a Habit?" *Hopes&Fears*, 20 Nov. 2015, www.hopesandfears.com/hopes/now/question/216479-how-long-does-it-really-take-to-break-a-habit.

11. "Earl Nightingale Quotes." Brainy-Quote.com. BrainyMedia Inc, 2019. 16 April 2019. https://www.brainyquote.com/quotes/earl_nightingale_390812

12. "myth." *Merriam-Webster.com*. Merri-am-Webster, 2018. Web. 17 October 2018.

13. Talks, TEDx, director. *YouTube. YouTube*, YouTube, 5 Dec. 2012, www.youtube.com/watch?v=AdKUJxjn-R8.

14. Evan Esar. 20,000 *Quips & Quotes*. (New York City, NY: Barnes & Noble Books, 1995).

15. Poem by Josh C. Jones

16. "Colin Powell Quotes." BrainyQuote.com. BrainyMedia Inc, 2018. 3 December 2018. https://www.brainyquote.com/quotes/colin_powell_138130

CHAPTER 6

CHARACTER

1. "Heraclitus Quotes." BrainyQuote.com. BrainyMedia Inc, 2019. 16 May 2019. https://www.brainyquote.com/quotes/heraclitus_397781

2. The Holy Bible, New International Version. Grand Rapids: Zondervan House, 1984. Print.

     a. Genesis 2:17

3. The Holy Bible, New International Version. Grand Rapids: Zondervan House, 1984. Print.

     a. Obadiah 1:3

4. The Holy Bible, New International Version. Grand Rapids: Zondervan House, 1984. Print.

   a. Philippians 4:8

5. The Holy Bible, New International Version. Grand Rapids: Zondervan House, 1984. Print.

   a. Romans 12:2

6. Dobbs, Michael. "SOVIET JOURNALISTS ATTACK KAL STORY." *The Washington Post*, WP Company, 26 May 1991, www.washingtonpost.com/archive/politics/1991/05/26/soviet-journalists-attack-kal-story/a0fab253-91f4-47e9-ada0-85d5b263d1df/?utm_term=.ec6da97f1646.

7. David Hoffman. *The Dead Hand: The Untold Story of the Cold War Arms Race and Its Dangerous Legacy*. First Anchor Books Edition. (New York, NY: Anchor Books, 2010).

8. "character." *Merriam-Webster.com.* Merriam-Webster, 2019. Web. 5 January 2019.

9. Mark Rutland. *Character Matters: Nine Essential Traits You Need to Succeed.* (Lake Mary, Florida: Charisma House, 2003).

10. Mark Rutland. *Character Matters: Nine Essential Traits You Need to Succeed.* (Lake Mary, Florida: Charisma House, 2003).

11. "Heraclitus Quotes." BrainyQuote.com. BrainyMedia Inc, 2022. 31 December 2022. https://www.brainyquote.com/quotes/heraclitus_117864

12. "Sanctify." *Merriam-Webster.com.* Merriam-Webster, 2021. Web. 8 February 2022.

13. The Holy Bible, New International Version. Grand Rapids: Zondervan House, 1984. Print.

    a. Romans 5:3-5

14. "The Science of Character." *Character Lives*, 10 May 2018, www.characterlives.

org/the-science-of-character/.

15. Neurosci. "Know Your Brain: Prefrontal Cortex." *Neuroscientifically Challenged*, Neuroscientifically Challenged, 18 May 2014, www.neuroscientificallychallenged.com/blog/2014/5/16/know-your-brain-prefrontal-cortex.

16. "John Wooden Quotes." BrainyQuote.com. BrainyMedia Inc, 2019. 20 February 2019. https://www.brainyquote.com/quotes/john_wooden_163015

17. "Abraham Lincoln Quotes." BrainyQuote.com. BrainyMedia Inc, 2019. 20 February 2019. https://www.brainyquote.com/quotes/abraham_lincoln_121094

18. Poem by Josh C. Jones

19. "Aaron Rodgers Quotes." BrainyQuote.com. BrainyMedia Inc, 2019. 7 March 2019. https://www.brainyquote.com/quotes/aaron_rodgers_833092

CHAPTER 7

DESTINY

1. "William Shakespeare Quotes." Brainy-Quote.com. BrainyMedia Inc, 2019. 10 July 2019. https://www.brainy-quote.com/quotes/william_shake-speare_101458

SPECIAL NOTE

Please remember that if you like a book or an author's work, the best thing you can do to help the message, story, or author is to tell others. You can also do this by leaving reviews and/or ratings on the online site where you purchased the material. By doing so, you help the book and/or author gain more exposure and reach more people. This is something that not all authors will express publicly, but all authors do hope the reader will graciously do, and we are appreciative and grateful for it.

Thank you.